TRACING YOUR EUROPEAN ROOTS

Volume V of *Quillen's Essentials of Genealogy*

2nd Edition

www.essentialgenealogy.com

PRAISE FOR DAN'S BOOKS

"*Mastering Online Genealogy* written by W. Daniel Quillen is a great little book packed full of helpful tips in doing online family research ... This informative book has some great tips for beginners, as well as those who have been doing research for a while ... I look forward to reading all of the books in this genealogical series." — *Tina Sansone, Bella Online book review*

"Your book *Secrets of Tracing your Ancestors* has been extremely helpful to me in a renewal of my genealogy interests." – *Nancy Dailey*

"I would like to thank you for writing a very informative book. There was a lot of information that I did not know about…" – *Donna Perryman Moon*

"I purchased your book and have found it most helpful." – *Glenda Laney*

"Thanks for your help and for writing your excellent book!" – *Laura Johnson*

"I have enjoyed reading your book and I've found excellent leads for finding ancestors." – *Donna Mann*

"… It is not only informative but entertaining. Incorporating your own experiences in brought the book to life. Again, thank you for helping me to understand the many aspects of genealogy and for supplying a roadmap to finding more information about our ancestors." – *Dana L. Hager*

"Of all the books I have looked at yours is the best…and you write with your heart and soul. Thanks for writing such a great book." – *Karen Dredge*

"I got this book out of the library, but before I was half-way through it, I decided I had to have my own copy. Lots of helpful suggestions! I'd recommend it for all new and experienced family historians." – *Margaret Combs*

"I am embarking on the family history journey and have found your book to be very helpful … thanks for putting together a helpful, easy to follow guide." – *Suzanne Adams*

"I'm absolutely delighted that I discovered your book "Secrets of Tracing Your Ancestors." I've only been at this for a month (to keep sane during knee surgery recuperation) and now I'm hooked." – *Cecily Bishop*

About the Author

For more than 20 years, W. Daniel Quillen has been a professional writer specializing in travel and technical subjects. He has taught beginning genealogy courses to university students and working adults, and is a frequent lecturer in beginning and intermediate genealogy classes in Colorado. He has compiled his years of genealogical training and research into a growing series of genealogy how-to books. He lives in Centennial, Colorado with his wife and children. If you would like to contact Dan about anything in this book, his e-mail address is: **wdanielquillen@gmail.com**.

TRACING YOUR EUROPEAN ROOTS

Volume V of *Quillen's Essentials of Genealogy*

2nd Edition

www.essentialgenealogy.com

W. Daniel Quillen

Author of *Secrets of Tracing Your Ancestors*; *The Troubleshooter's Guide to Do-It-Yourself Genealogy*; and *Quillen's Essentials of Genealogy* series

Cold Spring Press

COLD SPRING PRESS

Cold Spring Harbor, NY 11724
www.essentialgenealogy.com

2nd Edition

ISBN 13: 978-159360-175-1
Library of Congress Control Number: 2013938469

PHOTO CREDITS

Cover design by Matthew Simmons (www.myselfincluded.com). Back cover photo by Gilles Dubois from flickr.com.

If you want to contact the author directly, e-mail him at: wdanielquillen@gmail.com.

TABLE OF CONTENTS

1. INTRODUCTION

Willkomen! Benvenuto! Accueil! Bienvenida! Välkomnande! Welcome! Welcome to *Tracing Your European Roots*. America is truly the great Melting Pot, and the stew that is us consists of the descendants of German, Irish, French, English, Italian, etc., ancestors. In fact, in 2010, the US Census reported that Americans consisted of the following percentages of ancestral origins:

Nationality	Percentage
German	15.2%
African American	13.1%
Irish	12.1%
English	9.4%
Mexican	6.5%
American	6.1%
Italian	5.9%
Polish	3.3%
French	3.1%
American Indian	2.8%
Scottish	1.9%
Scotch-Irish	1.2%
Czechoslovakian	.9%
Portuguese	.5%
Total Population	307,006,556

Through the pages of this book, we'll investigate some of the places you can go to unearth (no pun intended – well, maybe a little) your European ancestors' records. I'll use the above census figures to guide our journey, starting with where to find the records of European ancestors, beginning with English records, Czech records, French records, and so on through the list.

Quillen's Essentials of Genealogy: Tracing Your European Roots is the fifth in a series of other *Essentials* books. One or more of the others in this series may come in handy for your research:

Mastering Online Genealogy

Mastering Immigration and Naturalization Records

Mastering Census and Military Records

Tracing Your Irish and British Roots.

Mastering Family, Library and Church Records

While each of those books represents a focused dive into various areas of genealogical research, one of the first two genealogy books I wrote might also prove useful to you:

Secrets of Tracing Your Ancestors – This book was originally targeted at beginning genealogists, although reviewers have noted that it contains sections, topics and tactics that are beneficial to beginning as well as more experienced researchers.

Troubleshooter's Guide to Do-It-Yourself Genealogy – This book is targeted at genealogists with a little more experience in genealogical research, perhaps those who have hit brick walls in their research and need a little extra help.

The *Quillen's Essentials of Genealogy* series as well as *Secrets* and the *Troubleshooter's Guide* are all published by Cold Spring Press.

Now that the shameless self-promotion is out of the way, we can get down to finding your European ancestors. However, before we jump into the records, let's talk about *The Basics*.

Since you picked up this book (thank you!), chances are your ancestors come from one or more of those countries. In fact – especially in Europe where most of those countries are about the size of US states (or smaller!), it is often the case that your family line may wend through several of those countries. As you pick up the thread of your family's origins, it may lead from one country to another to even a third or fourth European country. Because of that, I have chosen to provide information on numerous European countries in this book.

Through the following pages, we'll investigate some of the nooks and crannies you can search to find your European ancestors' records. So pack your virtual genealogical suitcase, and let's get started.

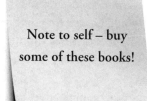

Note to self – buy
some of these books!

2. THE BASICS

Before you begin a cross-oceanic search for your ancestors, there are some research basics you should keep in mind. In *Secrets of Tracing your Ancestors*, I spend a good amount of time encouraging my readers to begin their genealogical research with the information they have at hand. What do your parents, grandparents, aunts, uncles and cousins know about the ancestor you are researching? Can they shed some light on the country your European ancestor came from, the town, city, state, province, region, etc? It would be well for you to glean every bit of information they have about your ancestors. Be cautious with this information (because some of it may be inaccurate!), but seek and record as much as possible.

Do any of your relatives have documents from your ancestors that may assist you? A birth certificate of your grandmother may tell you not only when and where she was born, but it may also tell you who her parents were (including her mother's maiden name), as well as their birth places. A marriage license for one of your ancestors who immigrated to America may provide a town or other geographic clue as to where she and her husband were married, and perhaps where they were born (people weren't as mobile as our society is today – they and their ancestors often lived and died within a very small town or region).

For researching my European ancestors, start at home!

See if you can glean the following information:

• Surname(s) of the individual(s) you are researching;

• Names of parents, siblings, spouses (including maiden names of women), etc.;

• County where they came from;

12

• Town, city, parish, province, region, etc. they lived in;
• Approximate years of critical events such as birth, death, marriage, etc.

This last bullet point, though seemingly innocuous, is important. You will be poring over records that may be hard for you to read and understand due to antiquated handwriting, a foreign language, terms you do not know, etc. If you have dates, even approximate ones, for the information you are seeking, that will help narrow your search in these difficult documents.

Understanding the history of your ancestors' country of nativity may help you weave slender threads of information into a beautiful tapestry that is your ancestor's life. For example, if your grandmother tells you that her grandfather came to America when he got tired of the bloody battles that kept happening in the part of Italy he was from, you may have just been given a clue that will help you find information about her grandfather. Knowing Italian history as you surely do, that tells you he may have been from southern Italy or perhaps even Sicily, and left as economic conditions worsened after the unification if Italy in 1861. That gives you an approximate timeframe to begin your search for him.

Patronymics
Since we are researching European roots, it is valuable for us to spend a short amount of time on patronymics – the practice of some peoples to use a name that identifies the named person with his or her father. I'll discuss a few of those here.

The Irish have their own form of patronymics recognized the world over. Prefixes such as Mc or Mac were used to signify the *son of:* McDonnell was therefore the son of Donnell. Another prefix was the O' which meant "descended from," and a grandson or great grandson might use such a prefix. Occasionally the English passed laws to annoy the Irish (actually, they were trying to assimilate them into English culture). One such law forbade the use of the patronymics *O* and *Mc*. At that time, the patronymic *fitz* replaced *Mc* for son of: Fitzmorris then meant the son of Morris.

Even more prevalent than Irish patronymics are Scandinavian patronymics. I suppose we all know more than our fair share of individuals with surnames like Anderson (Anders' son) and Johnson (John's son). For centuries Scandinavians employed this naming scheme, and until surnames became common (in the late 1700s or early 1800s depending on the location), the names changed from generation to generation.

The Jewish culture also has its patronymics. You will occasionally see the name *ben* used to designate the son of, as in David *ben* Joseph (David, the son of Joseph). Certain Jewish groups also used patronymics to honor living grandparents, and there was a specific order used to designate names. The first-born son was often named after his paternal grandfather, and his brother (the second son) was named after his maternal grandfather. They used this practice for their daughters too: first-born daughters were given the name of their paternal grandmother and second-born daughters received the names of their maternal grandmother. This method of naming was especially popular with Sephardic Jews.

The French adopted the term fitz to mean son of: Fitzpatrick was therefore the son of Patrick (fitz was derived from the French work *fils*, which means son).

Spanish surnames are often derived from patronymics. In Spain and Portugal, an abbreviated way to identify a person with his or her father was by the addition of *az, ez, iz,* or *oz* to their father's last name. For instance, Julio, el hijo de Rodrigo became Julio Rodriquez (Julio, the son of Rodrigo).

Spelling Woes

Here's a hint that is probably heresy to my 6th grade teacher: Don't limit yourself to only one spelling of your name. In my research, in nearly every one of my family lines, at one time or another I have found variations in the spelling – sometimes within the same generation! Here are a few examples from my own family:

Sellers, Sellars, Sellar
Ritchie, Ritchey, Richey

DON'T DO IT!

I can almost guarantee you that at some time or other in your research you will run across information that you'll "know" just isn't right. The temptation will be to correct the information rather than just write down what you have found.

Don't do it!

Perhaps it's the first name of an ancestor. While you might be absolutely certain that your great-great grandmother's name is Theodora, if you find her listed in a US Census as "Dolly," that is the name you should record as you copy the data down. Or perhaps it's your last name that has been spelled creatively. Resist the temptation to substitute the information that is different. Copy the record exactly as you find it so that you can have an accurate representation of what you found.

Horney, Harney
Quillan, Quillen, Quillon, Quillin, McQuillan, McQuillon, etc.
Lowrance/Lorentz
McCollough/McCullough
Rogers/Rodgers
Throckmorton, Throgmorton
Hudson/Hutson
Graham/Grimes

And just because you are a Smith or a Jones (by the way - is it true that the surname of Adam and Eve was Jones?), don't assume you are immune from spelling changes: Smith / Smythe / Smithy / Schmidt or Jones / Jonas/ Joans, etc.

I have a very fresh example of the need to be open to name variations. As I was writing this book, I was in correspondence with a niece of mine who was researching her father's family, a group of Germans who settled in Russia near the Volga River. Her maiden name is Behm, and she discovered that the German name *Böhm* was often spelled *Boehm*, and the variation of *Behm*

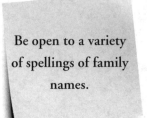

Be open to a variety of spellings of family names.

from *Boehm* was not a far-fetched idea. All this she accepted. There were no online or microfilm census records for the areas her relatives lived, but through a lot of digging on the Internet, she found a source that was selling copies of the 1832 and 1864 censuses that would have included the Volga River German enclave her ancestors were a part of. She talked her father and sister into splitting the cost of the censuses and she ordered them.

She was so excited to search the censuses for her ancestor Henry Behm / Boehm / Böhm. The day came that the census arrived, and she feverishly checked the families and was at first delighted to see many Böhm families. But – alas, not one single Henry among them. She was heartbroken and distraught. My sister shared her daughter's frustrations – there were plenty of Heinrichs, but not a single Henry! I gently pointed out that in 1832 Germany there wouldn't have been anyone named Henry – they would have only been named *Heinrich*! Joy returned to my niece and her family.

There are many reasons for variation of name spellings, and your creative detective work will have to gather all the threads together into one cohesive answer. Immigration officials are often accused of this, but in my opinion that happened far less than was alleged. The name change may have been due to an immigration official, or it may have been illiteracy. Another reason might be that the newly immigrated family wanted to fit in to their new country. In that case, Meier became Meyer, Schneider became Snider, Schmidt became Smith and Blau became Blue. In my family, McQuillan became Quillan.

Before we get too far along this genealogical journey we're taking together, let's take a few minutes and set the stage for searching for your European ancestors. There are many records available to assist your research. I have found that it usually takes multiple records to yield the information I am looking for. One document sheds light in one area, which leads me to another, which confirms the previous data and provides me with more data.

Tiny clues are hidden in countless records, clues that initially may not seem to be important, but which may later prove to be just the item of information needed to solve a mystery.

The goal, of course, is to find the genealogical information for an ancestor and their family. As you discover a birth date and birth place in records closer to home (immigration or census records, for example), those will lead you to the land of nativity for your ancestor. Further searches in the land of their nativity will likely confirm information reported on the immigration or naturalization record, uncover other family members, and assist you in moving further along on your pedigree chart, pushing it ever up the family tree, further and further back in time.

To be the most efficient in your search, first gather all the information you know about your ancestor. Speak with living parents, grandparents, aunts and uncles, cousins, etc. One of them may recall information that will become important to your search. Maybe they recall that one of your ancestors mentioned how beautiful Boston was when they stepped off the ship bringing them to America. Or perhaps they remember that great grandpa mentioned he had 3 lire in his pockets when he stepped off the ship in America.

United States Records First. Often, information that will help you in your search for immigrant ancestors will be information found in United States. A census record that lists your ancestor may list him or her under a name you didn't realize they went by. As an example, the 1920 census lists my great grandmother as Dolly. Her full name was Theodora Charity McCollough, but the name she went by was Dolly. So a search of a census, immigration or naturalization record might not turn her up if you search for Theodora Charity McCollough Quillen. At a minimum, I should search under Theodora, Charity and Dolly. A death certificate, tombstone, obituary or other very US record may well reveal information I did not know, but information that will help me pinpoint her later on in other records.

What's in a Name? Further to the discussion above — do you know your ancestors' given as well as surnames? Knowing their given names – all of them – may help you sort out your ancestor from millions of others. Perhaps he or she went by a middle or christening name. While you might be unable to locate your ancestor Johannes Schmidt in records, you might discover a Wilhelm Schmidt who immigrated to the US. Johannes Wilhelm Schmidt, like the author of this book, just happened to go by his middle name, not his first name.

As mentioned above in the example about my great grandmother, Theodora Charity Quillen, I'd do well to be open to diminutives (Timmy for Tim, Billy or Willy for William, etc.) as well as other possible nicknames as I scour records in search of her.

Know Your History. Knowing a little of the history of your family as well as their native country may also help you pin down that immigrant ancestor of yours. If family tradition is that your second great grandfather came to America during the *Great Potato Famine* in Ireland, then that narrows your search for other records to a manageable half dozen years or so – 1845 to 1852. During that time period, a blight hit the potatoes of Ireland, rotting them in the ground. Potatoes were the main staple for the Irish diet, and it is estimated that approximately one million souls perished as a result. In addition, approximately another million Irish immigrated from Ireland during this time, the majority of which came to America.

One of my wife's ancestors is from Germany. Family tradition holds that as it looked like Germany was headed into what has become known as The Great War (World War I), her second great grandmother packed her four military-age sons off to America to get them out of harm's way. That tells me I should search for their immigration records in the years leading up to the war's outbreak in 1914.

So – pay attention to history!

Ethnic Gatherings. Often, immigrants coming to America were coming to join other family members or neighbors. As you search for your immigrant ancestors, be aware of where large populations of their ethnic group may have settled. Swedes ended up in Minnesota, the Irish centered in Boston and New York, the Polish in Chicago, Italians in New York and Chicago, even Bulgarians in New Mexico. (Bet you didn't know that!) While stereotypes or assumptions such as these may not apply to your ancestors, you cannot afford to overlook the possibility. Had I Irish ancestors (I do – lucky me!), I would be sure and search immigration records for Boston and New York. Could they have entered the US someplace else? Of course. But as a starting point, these ports of entry make the most sense if I have nothing better to go on.

Religion. You ask why religious affiliation should be considered? Well, because sometimes like-minded religionists immigrated to the US at the same time. Look at the founding of our country, which started with a colony of Pilgrims who came to America aboard the Mayflower, followed by the Puritans. Many early Pennsylvania pioneers were Quakers. If your ancestors came from Ireland, they're sure to be Catholic, right? Well, maybe – remember that the area that is now Northern Ireland was once "planted" by the Queen Elizabeth with Protestants during the late 16th and 17th centuries (there's that history thing again!). Searching Catholic baptismal records for an ancestor from the six northern counties of Ireland might prove fruitless.

A Few Helpful Items. I consider myself a pretty experienced researcher. But truth be told (and I always tell the truth!), much of the research I have done has been in America or in English-speaking foreign countries – primarily Ireland and England. I am here to tell you that your first ventures into foreign records that are in a language other than English will be startling. Adding to the difficulty will be unfamiliar handwriting – whether elegant cursive or barely legible scribbling, you may find the going difficult.

In the following country-specific chapters, in addition to covering sources of genealogical research and records, I have provided some get-you-started words that you will likely encounter during your research. I have provided the words you are likely to run into in genealogical records – birth, baptism / confirmation, death, marriage, etc. I've also provided the names of the month, but you may feel that's unnecessary. Consider the names of the month in **German**:

Januar
Februar

Marz
Abril
Mai
Juni
Juli
August
September
Oktober
November
Dezember

Aside from the fact I listed them in consecutive order, I doubt any of us would have a difficult time recognizing the months of the year in German. **French** is perhaps a little more difficult:

Janvier
Février
Mars
Avril
Mai
Juin
Juillet
Août
Setembre
Octobre
Novembre
Décembre

Still, not too bad. June, July and August might cause a momentary pause, but generally not too bad. But if you are doing research in the **Czech Republic**, you'll be very happy to have my assistance on this point:

Leden – January

Únor – February

Březen – March

Duben – April

Květen – May

Červen – June

Červenec – July

Srpen – August

Září – September

Říjen – October

Listopadu – November

Prosince – December

A little different. And don't even get me started on the names of the month in Polish!

Hopefully these will help you navigate your way through the maze of unfamiliar words so you are able to get the most out of these records once you locate them.

In addition, I have included names that are common to the country being discussed. In my own research, knowledge of the correct spelling of names – first as well as surnames – has allowed me to decipher many a nearly illegible scrawl of a name on a census record or marriage certificate.

As you begin your journey among foreign-language documents, prepare yourself for a little culture shock. Your brain will likely feel overwhelmed with these strange symbols as well as antiquated and flourish-filled hand-writing. But don't despair. Those I have spoken with who spend great amounts of time with European documents assure me that in time, you will become accustomed to the differences.

That being said, it's a good idea to seek out books that will assist you in learning the script of the nation whose records you are perusing. There are many on the market. An excellent book to assist when you are researching European records is *Following the Paper Trail: A Multilingual Translation Guide* by Jonathan D. Shea and William F. Hoffman (Avotaynu, Inc., Teaneck, New Jersey, 1994). Although it is a little dated, the information – from a genealogical assistance standpoint – is timeless. History of many of the European languages, writing samples, examples of typical birth, death, marriage certificates, and passport applications all help you to take a guided tour through these information-laden documents.

Here are three hints that may help you decipher some of those difficult handwritten records:

1. If a particular letter in a given or surname is undecipherable, or could be one of several letters, scan the rest of the document looking for the same (or similar) letters in words you already know. If you know the correct spelling of one of the words used elsewhere, you may be able to see how the writer formed that particular letter, and that will help you decipher the name you're having difficulty with.

2. There's no substitute for experience. I guarantee you that the first few handwritten records you work with will seem a daunting challenge. But the more you work with them, the easier it becomes. Don't give up – give yourself a chance to study, review, read and re-read. It will come.

3. Realize that at the end of the day, there will be records that you (nor anyone else) simply may not be able to decipher due to poor quality of a text, poor handwriting, etc. Copy the information as best you can (take a picture or copy of the document if you are able), and continue your search.

3. CLUES & HINTS

Before you jump on your computer and book a flight to your ancestor's land of nativity across the Big Pond – *Stop*! There are many sources and records in the United States you can use to pinpoint your ancestor in that European country you're just itching to visit. In fact, while the information from US sources may help you find these European ancestors of yours, they may be downright critical in pinpointing their exact location. If you shun these sources, you may find yourself getting to the land of your ancestors' nativity, only to realize you wish you had more information – where did they live and die? What town were they from? What parish church did they attend, and where are *their* forebears buried?

In this chapter, we'll explore some of the sources available to you here in the United States, many accessible from your home office, bedroom, family room – where ever your computer is located.

Family Tradition / Legend / Knowledge

Often it is wise to listen to the family traditions about where great grandma and grandpa came from. Sometimes, however, you need to take this information with a grain (or a box) of salt. I have run into this in my own family. My dear great grandmother was a bit of a genealogist. If you have read any of my other books, you may recall that she completed the center section of the family Bible with genealogies of her and her husband's families. Some of her information goes back to the 1700s.

However, several times I have found myself running headlong down wrong paths because I took at face value what she had written. Her great, great grandmother, it turns out, was not of Scotch descent as her record indicates, but she was actually from Ireland, as were several generations of her immediate forebears. Perhaps that German second great grandfather of yours came from Germany. Or Poland. Or France. Or….? Knowing and understanding the histories of some of those countries and the movement of their borders may help you locate information on your ancestors.

Use this information as a starting point, not as the gospel truth. You may find the stories and traditions handed down for the past 150 to 200 years are spot-on accurate, but then again, you may find a bit of variation from the real story. At least be open to that possibility.

Immigration & Naturalization Records
Some of the most valuable records for helping pinpoint the homes of your European ancestors may well come from the immigration and naturalization records kept by the United States government. These voluminous records shed immense light on our nation's immigrant arrivals.

Immigration records refer to those records that detail information about your ancestors' journeys to America. They include:

1. Ship passenger lists – these are the rosters of all who traveled on a particular ship to the United States. They are sometimes called *ship manifests*. These records, especially in later immigration years, contain a great deal of information of genealogical value.

2. Certificates of arrival – these were short notices containing the immigrant's name, date of departure and arrival, ports of departure and entry and the name of the ship on which they traveled. Very little information of genealogical value is to be found on Certificates of Arrival, but they may lead you to other more helpful documents.

3. Censuses – censuses taken in later years after an immigrants' arrival may contain valuable clues to finding immigration and naturalization papers completed by the immigrant. The census itself is full of genealogical value, but may lead you to other documents that will expand that information exponentially.

Naturalization records refer to those records immigrants completed to become US citizens. There are several:

4. **Declaration of Intent** – these were papers completed to indicate the immigrant's intention to become a US citizen. They were often completed immediately upon arrival in the United States, but were sometimes completed later. These are often called *first papers*. These papers usually have a great deal of genealogical information in them, including birth dates and places of birth for the immigrant and his family.

5. **Petition for Naturalization** – these papers were completed by the immigrant as part of his or her formal request to become a United States citizen. Generally speaking, Petitions for Naturalization could not be completed until an immigrant had been in the United States at least five years. They are also called *second papers* or *final papers*, as well as *Petition for Citizenship*. These papers usually have a great deal of genealogical information in them.

6. **Oath of Allegiance** – this is the document the immigrant signs as s/he becomes a citizen of the United States, renouncing his allegiance to any other foreign power, dignitary, king, etc. Very little information of a genealogical value is contained in Oaths of Allegiance, but there may be some clues that will lead you to other sources of information.

Emigration records are records kept at the location where your ancestor embarked on a ship to come to America. Sometimes they provide significant information, sometimes they do not. Don't overlook them when searching for your immigrant ancestors.

The second book in the *Quillen's Essentials of Genealogy* series is *Mastering Immigration and Naturalization Records* and it takes a much more focused look at these valuable records – about 144 pages' worth.

United States Census Records
In the first chapter I mentioned that the book that precedes this one in the *Quillen's Essentials of Genealogy* series is *Mastering Census and Military Records*. That book goes into great depth on the United States censuses. A portion of that book addresses how the census can assist you in identifying your ancestors' land of nativity. I'll hit some of the high points as they relate to your European ancestors here.

From very early in our country's history, Lady Liberty was interested in where her citizens were born, and the land of their parents' nativity. Following are the questions asked about birth in the various censuses that may be an assist to you in finding your European ancestors:

1820
• Foreigners not naturalized

1850
• Birthplace

1860
• Birthplace

1870
• Birthplace
• Father foreign born
• Mother foreign born

1880
• Place of birth
• Place of birth of father
• Place of birth of mother

1890 — Enumeration date 1 June 1890
Note: Tragically, the vast majority of the 1890 Census was destroyed in a fire (or by the water that was used to put out the fire!).

1900
• Place of birth
• Place of birth of father
• Place of birth of mother

1910
• Place of birth
• Place of birth of father
• Place of birth of mother

1920
- Place of birth
- Mother tongue
- Place of birth of father
- Mother tongue of father
- Place of birth of mother
- Mother tongue of mother

1930
- Place of birth
- Place of birth of father
- Place of birth of mother
- Mother tongue (or native language) if foreign born

1940
- Place of birth
- Citizenship of the foreign born
- Place of birth of father
- Place of birth of mother
- Mother tongue (or native language) if foreign born
- Citizenship of the foreign born?

Note some of the important questions that were added in the 1920, 1930 and 1940 censuses – in addition to asking about the birth place of the individual and his / her parents, they also asked about the mother tongue of that person as well as that person's parents.

The question that first appears in the 1940 census: *Citizenship of the foreign born?* may also provide a clue for your research.

This information may be a great assist as you unravel your ancestors' history. A great grandparent who speaks Spanish could be from Spain, Mexico, or many countries in Central and South America. (or was it really Portuguese that she spoke?!) These and similar questions may lead you to the right country.

Don't overlook censuses, immigration and naturalization records for clues!

In addition to the questions regarding country of birth, the federal censuses for 1900, 1910, 1920 and 1930 each asked a series of questions that may provide clues to assist you in finding these ocean-going ancestors of yours. These censuses all asked whether a person had been naturalized, along with other helpful questions. The 1920 census went a step further by requiring the year of naturalization. That last will be especially helpful, and will assist you in locating your ancestor's naturalization papers. By census, here are the immigration and naturalization questions asked:

1900
• If an immigrant, the year of immigration to the United States.
• How long the immigrant has been in the United States.
• Is the person naturalized?

1910
•Year of immigration to the United States
•Whether naturalized or alien
• Whether able to speak English, or, if not, give language spoken.

1920
•Year of immigration to the United States
•Naturalized or alien
•If naturalized, year of naturalization

1930
•Year of immigration into the United States
•Naturalization
• Whether able to speak English

In the *Citizenship* column of these censuses, where the above questions were asked, these abbreviations were used: AL = Alien, NA = Naturalized, NR = Not Reported, PA = First Papers filed (the immigrant's declaration of intention).

Passport Applications
American travelers abroad have been applying for passports since 1789. Travel between the United States and Europe was frequent during the 19th

century, and perhaps one of those travelers was an ancestor of yours. Individuals and families returned to their former homes in Europe to vacation, take care of businesses that had been left in the old country, retrieve family members left behind, and to settle estates. And probably many, many more reasons.

The applications they left behind often provide basic genealogical data such as their full name, birth date, and their place of birth (sometimes just the country, but more often than not the country and town). Often, as an added bonus, physical descriptions were included on the passports.

The vast majority of 19th century passports were for men – their wives and children often traveled on his passport. Information was generally added to his passport identifying the individuals, their relationship to the man, their names and ages.

Histories / Biographies

In the latter half of the 19th century and the beginning of the 20th century, city, county and even state histories were popular. An important part of these histories was the biography of the county's / city's / town's "leading citizens." Often, these biographies will shed tremendous light on your ancestors.

Before I go further, let me explain that *leading citizens* may have been some of the county's oldest residents – their pioneers, if you will. They may have been those active in politics – mayors, governors, etc. Or simply those who were willing to pay a small fee to have their story told in the pages of the book. These latter biographical subjects may have been every-day people: farmers, dairy men, blacksmiths or store keepers. Following is a short excerpt about a neighbor of my fourth great grandfather's, whose life was captured in *Biographies of Old Schuyler County (Illinois) Settlers*, written in 1878:

WILLIAM DEAN

William Dean was born in County Dennygaul, Ireland, May 3d, 1825, and is a son of John Dean. He received his early education in the district schools of Ireland. At about the age of twenty-two he emigrated to America, landing in New York. From there he went to the western part of Pennsylvania, where he resided two years. He then moved to Schuyler county, Illinois, in the spring of 1850, where he engaged in farming. In March, 1857, he was married to Mrs. Maria Pain, daughter of George and Jane Humphreys; she was born July 10th, 1830. The fruits of their marriage is a family of four children, one of whom is now deceased. Mr. Dean is at present residing on his farm in Littleton township, enjoying good health.

Information from this short biography shares important information about this Irish gentleman, information I might not otherwise find. Were he my ancestor, before I headed for Ireland, I would have a much more focused area in which to look — County Dennygaul (knowing the counties in Ireland and the Irish brogue as I do, I am sure this refers to County Donegal – on the northwest coast of Ireland) — as opposed to trying to scour the whole of Ireland in search of information about William Dean. Also, the details of his arrival date, age at arrival and subsequent movements within America give me clues to uncovering other documents – immigration and naturalization records, censuses, etc., that will help me further refine my search for William Dean and his ancestors.

Once you've researched these clues and narrowed your search as finely as possible, it's time to begin searching the records from the land of your ancestors' nativity. Again, rather than jump on a plane headed for Germany, for example, to search the records there, be sure to check for records that might be available from the comfort of your home office. Many are online, and many more are coming online daily. The following chapters will address many of those records.

4. RESEARCH TOOLS

Rather than repeat this information through each country's research section, I will provide an overview of various research sources that can be used across each of the countries covered in this book. Doing so allows me to concentrate more information in each of the country-specific sections.

Ancestry.com

Ancestry.com is one of the most recognized search tools available to genealogists. It is also one of the most useful and has a significant number of collections online — they boast over 7 billion records are in their various collections, about a billion of which are for foreign countries. Since this is a book about European research, if you use Ancestry.com for finding your European ancestors, you'll need to purchase their international package. As of this writing, the cost for the international package (which includes domestic collections) is:

Worldwide Deluxe Membership
Annual — $299.40
Six-month — $169
One month — $34.95

Are you intrigued about the possibility, but not sure you're willing to take the big leap? Then perhaps you spend $35 and try it for one month. Or, an option I have used has been a two-week free trial. This will give you a flavor of the records available, the ease of navigation, user-friendliness of the service, etc. In the past, Ancestry.com allowed quarterly subscriptions, but unfortunately that is no longer an option – very disappointing. So if you're like me and do genealogy in stops and starts, the monthly subscription may be best for you.

Books

Often, you'll be able to find books that will be of great assistance in your genealogical research. For example, you'll be amazed at the variety and differences in language you'll encounter as you begin researching foreign documents. A book on Polish handwriting, for example, may be a great assist to you as you begin poring over ancient Polish records that you run across on a website.

Earlier, I mentioned the book *Following the Paper Trail: A Multilingual Translation Guide* by Jonathan D. Shea and William F. Hoffman. If you are venturing into European countries in search of your ancestors for the first time, I strongly suggest getting your hands on this book. In addition, don't overlook books that may have been written about your specific branch of the family. The Internet makes searching quick and easy – you probably don't even have to go to your local library. Use Google to search for books about any of your ancestors. Perhaps someone has written a book entitled: *The McQuillan Clan of Ireland, McCollough Clans of Scotland,* or *The Rodriquez Family of Portugal.* It's not necessary to reinvent the proverbial ancestral wheel as you begin your research. Be sure and consider all sources that may point you further up the ancestral tree.

Country- and record-specific websites

The Internet is an incredible tool for doing genealogy, and it is especially so as you begin researching in Europe. Use it to find websites specific to the country – even specific to the type record you are seeking. Google *Ireland genealogy* or *Ireland marriages genealogy,* for example, and then pick and choose the websites that are most relevant to your search. You may need to narrow the number down by specifying a city or region of the country. Note that when you are looking for birth, death and marriage records, add the word *genealogy* to your search string and that helps eliminate the websites that cover getting current birth, death and marriage records.

CyndisList.com

Cyndi's List has been a great site for genealogists since its inception in 1996. It's a potpourri of links to great genealogical information. From the Home page, select *Categories* and then search for the country you are interested in.

Cyndi's List is free, although many of her links lead you to subscription-based services.

FamilySearch.org

Through the years, I have used FamilySearch.org extensively for my research and have been very pleased with the information I have been able to find in this tremendous genealogical website. It is provided by the Church of Jesus Christ of Latter-day Saints – the LDS Church. Unlike Ancestry.com or other subscription services, FamilySearch.org is free. A busy website (last estimate was that it receives nearly 5 million hits daily!), it is also relatively easy to navigate, once you get used to it.

Most of my use of FamilySearch.org has been for US research. However, they also have extensive international collections, and these collections are growing all the time. They also have a very good tutorial section. Some of the records in their collections have been digitized. Some of the records have been transcribed. Many (most) of the records held by the LDS Church have been put on microfilm or microfiche, and are not available online. They can be ordered for a small (postage) fee and delivered to any of over 4,500 Family History Centers located in over 130 countries. These Family History Centers are located in local LDS church meetinghouses – probably right in your neighborhood!

FreeTranslation.com

I daresay if you use this website once, you will use it many times. It is particularly helpful as you do research in countries where you are not fluent in the native tongue of the country. A word or phrase can be entered and translated online. As I have studied records from various countries, this website has been an invaluable assist to me. Since this is a book on searching for your European ancestors, you'll be pleased to know that this website provides translation services for all the countries we'll be covering in this book. As you'll read in the next paragraph, this site isn't as adept at translating large blocks of data as Google Translate is. You can find this site at *www.freetranslation.com.*

Google Translate

I have used *www.freetranslation.com* for many years and like it. But I am rapidly becoming converted to another translation website: Google Translate (*www.translate.google.com*). It seems as responsive and correct as freetranslation.com, but it handles large blocks of data far better than freetranslation.com. This is especially helpful if you run across an international website that doesn't have translation capability built in. You can copy many paragraphs of data at one time and paste into Google Translate for an immediate translation.

Genealogy Societies

Country-specific genealogy societies can be great resources in your search for your European ancestors. Just Google *German genealogy society, Irish genealogy society, French genealogy society*, etc. You'll be able to benefit from the research these groups have done. Often, they have put records online, identified worthwhile websites and provided valuable tips and tricks that will help you further research on your European ancestors. I perused several of these sites while writing this book and was impressed with the range of services provided by many different genealogy societies.

Google

Don't forget good ol' Google in your search for your ancestors! Sometimes I find myself caught up in researching using various and sundry genealogy-focused websites, such as Ancestry.com, FamilySearch.org, CyndisList, etc., and forget that Google (and Yahoo, Bing, etc.) can also be an effective genealogy search engine. If you are looking for marriage information on your great grandparents, who were married in Germany, simply try typing *German Marriage Records* into the Google search box. The more information you can include, such as town or German state, will help refine your search to a manageable number of sites.

Okay – we're set. It's time to strap on your seatbelts and hit the metaphoric road, and begin your search of those European ancestors. The chapters following will introduce you to the basics of researching records for a variety of European nations. These include Britain, Czechoslovakia, France, Germany, Ireland, Italy, Poland, Portugal and Spain.

Coverage of Britain and Ireland are somewhat brief compared to the coverage both countries will receive in the next *Essentials* book: *Tracing Your Irish and British Roots*. But these chapters will get you started. (I'll try to do more than merely whet your appetite!)

Find a translation website I like and am comfortable with.

5. YOUR BRITISH ROOTS

One advantage you will have – or so you would think – when doing British research, is that the records will all be in English. Unlike research you may do in other countries, you will not have to learn a new language, or at least enough words to identify genealogically significant words. Notwithstanding that bonus, old English records can be nearly as difficult to read as records in other languages, owing to archaic spelling, Gothic handwriting, etc. But – still, you should be thankful you don't have to bridge the language barrier in addition to the archaic usage and script stumbling blocks.

In the 2010 US census of the United States, nearly twenty-nine million Americans indicated they were of British descent. That number only trailed

SEPARATED BY A COMMON LANGUAGE

When my wife and I visited long-lost cousins in Northern Ireland, we had a delightful time. As we were leaving, one of the cousins took my wife's hand, and shaking it vigorously, said, "We're so glad you came. You are so plain and homely." For a moment we were both stunned by this seemingly insulting comment. But the broad smile on her face and the enthusiastic nods of agreement from the other Irish cousins present made us realize that in American English she was saying: "We're so glad you came. You are so down-to-earth and comfortable to be with."

That experience reinforced for us the fact that while we share a similar language with that part of the world, there are some distinct differences. (Note – the above was borrowed from another of the books written by the author – *Ireland Guide*, Open Road Publishing, 2006 – alas, now out of print!).

German, African-American and Irish ancestry. So if you are of English extraction, you appear to be in good (and plentiful) company.

Key Records
There are a number of key records available as you begin your search for your British roots. Following are some of those sources:

Censuses
Like their American cousins, the British have conducted censuses every ten years since the beginning of the 19th century (the Americans began at the end of the 18th century, with the 1790 census). Censuses were enumerated every ten years beginning in 1801. For some reason, they didn't complete a 1941 survey (they were a little busy / preoccupied at the time!). That's a shame, since everyone in America has been thrilled with the release of the 1940 census here.

For those of you who have become familiar with doing research with US censuses, you know they can be a great assist to genealogical research. The same holds true for research in Britain, however, there are some important differences between US and British censuses. Following are some of the primary differences:

- **Questions** — the questions are similar, but different. The main questions are the same: name, relationship to the head of household, age (there's a caveat here — see below), place of birth, etc.
- **1801 to 1831 censuses** – Many of the census records for these years were lost or destroyed. When there is information, it is like the US censuses between 1790 and 1840 – tallies of family members under the name of the head of household. Sometimes, the only information that survived for some areas are tallies – no names.
- **Dates of enumeration** – British censuses were taken in the second year of each decade: 1841, 1851, etc. Enumerations were generally in the April / May timeframe of those years.
- **Release date** — in the US, censuses are released to the public 72 years after they were enumerated; in Britain, censuses are only released after 100 years. That means the latest census available for awhile is the 1911 census, which was recently released.

37

- **Age** – in the US, the age of each individual is included. In Britain, the ages of those over 15 years of age are rounded to the nearest five years. So a family with children ages 15, 17 and 19 could show them as aged 15, 15 and 20. (Note – this was the instruction for enumerators, but I have reviewed many British census records, and many of them appear to have the exact (unrounded) age. But I am always suspicious of dates that are in fact multiples of 5 – not knowing for certain whether that was a person's real age or rounded age.
- **Indexes** – Indexes are not always readily available for the British censuses. It seems to be driven by the service you are working with. Ancestry.com, for example, has indexes available for the 1841 through 1901 censuses. British Origins, however, only had 1841, 1861, and 1871 indexes available.
- **All persons** – The first British census to list all individuals in a household by name was the 1841 census. (In the US, the first census to list all individuals was 1850, so the Brits are ahead of us on that one!) British censuses prior to that simply provide tallies of the household under the head of household name, similar to the US censuses prior to 1850.

British census terms you may not know:

- **Stray** – a person appearing in a record who is not from the place of enumeration.
- **Summary Books** – sometimes you'll run into Summary Books. These books just provide the name of the head of house with how many males and females are also living in the house, similar to US censuses from 1790 to 1840, except age ranges are not listed.
- **Workhouse** – a house built specifically to house poor or destitute people.

Where to Find British Census Records

Like US records, British census records continue to come online. Some of the best places I have found to find British census records are at Ancestry.com, Britishorigins.com and FamilySearch.org. There are often other places available – just Google *England Census online*, along with the name of a city or other location.

Civil Registration

Civil registration of birth, marriage and deaths began July 1, 1837. Indexes for these superb records are kept in book form in the Family Records Centre in London. You can see an index of the records they have at *www.findmypast.co.uk*. Records are also available at *freepages.genealogy.rootsweb.ancestry.com/ -thecohens/birthindexes-bri.html*. The former website is a subscription service, but the latter is free. I'd suggest you start with the last one! FamilySearch.org also has many of these records online. Many are transcribed, some have images available, and still others have links to pay-per-view or subscription partners.

Parish Registers

Prior to the beginning of civil registration (which officially began on July 1, 1837), the primary vital records were kept by the Church of England (which you'll recall, was the official established church in England). Between 1754 and 1837, the only marriages recognized by the Crown government were those marriages performed in the Church of England. Even though your ancestors may not have been Church of England members, if they wanted to be legally married, they had to do so in the Church of England. The only exceptions granted were for Jews and Quakers. Burials of non-Church of England members were also often recorded in Church of England records if the individual's church (called non-conformist churches, or the Catholic Church) didn't have burial grounds.

If you recall your history, King Henry VIII separated from the Catholic Church in 1534 and established the Church of England. The earliest Church of England parish records date to 1535. Even though civil registration began in 1837, many vital records are still kept by the Church of England. Prior to 1754, baptisms, burials and marriages were all kept in the same record. In 1754, marriage records were required to be kept in separate records, and in 1812, burials and baptisms were required to be kept in their own set of records.

Because of their popularity with genealogical researchers, many parish records have found their way online, obviating the need for a trip to England. But that's okay – there are still many parish records that are not online, and can be viewed only in England!

Wills and Probate Records

England offers a rich supply of wills and probate records. These records extend well into the history of England – some being as old as 1,000 years old!

Registration Districts

For genealogical research between 1837 and 1874, registration districts are one of the first bits of geographical information you'll need to locate your British ancestor's information. You can determine the registration district a particular county or parish was in by going to *www.ukbmd.org.uk/genuki/places/index.html*. That website allows you to search alphabetically by registration district or parish.

Helpful Websites for British Research

Following are websites that will be helpful as you venture into the British Isles in search of your ancestors:

Ancestry.com

Ancestry.com's international subscription edition includes an extensive British collection, including nearly 200 collections, such as:

• United Kingdom and Ireland obituary collection
• England and Wales birth index 1837 to 1915
• England and Wales marriage index 1916 to 2005
• England and Wales Censuses (1841 to 1901)
• London marriage banns, 1754 to 1921

British Origins — *www.britishorigins.com*. This is one of the early entries into the British genealogy subscription services website race, and I really like them. They offer access to over 70 million British records that range from 1209 to 1948 – that's a wide range of years! Their records include censuses, wills, birth, marriage and death certificates, burial and cemetery records, etc. British Origins allows 72-hour, monthly and annual subscriptions. You can get a combined British and Irish subscription or if you're only interested in British genealogy, you can get an British-only subscription. Costs as of this writing are:

	72-hour	Monthly	Annual
British only	£7.00	£9.50	(not available)
Irish only	£6.00	£9.50	(not available)
Combination	£8.00	£10.50	£55.00

(Note these prices are in British pounds (£), not euros or dollars. As of this writing, the conversion rate is $1.60 per £1. So £7 ~ $11.20.)

Following is a sampling of the collections available through British Origins:

- England and Wales 1841 census
- England and Wales 1861 census
- England and Wales 1871 census
- Dorsey, Surrey and London marriage records, 1500 through 1856
- York marriage bonds, 1613 to 1839
- National Wills index

And that's all just a sampling. Doesn't it just make you want to dive right in?

Find My Past – *www.findmypast.co.uk* is another of the British services available to research your British ancestors. They offer subscription services (£69.95 for six months, £109.95 for one year) or you can purchase credits you can then use on a pay-per-view system. Credits cost £24.95 for 280 credits, and must be used within one year. Or you can get 60 credits for £6.95, and those must be used within 90 days. Records cost 5 to 30 credits (most in the 5- to 10-credit range) to view, depending on the record.

FamilySearch.org – *www.familysearch.org* has a number of documents and videos courses about British research, and all are available to the public for free. I found two great video courses that were helpful in learning and understanding British research. They are located at *https://www.familysearch.org/learningcenter/results.html?q=british%20research.* They represented a short beginner's series; the first is called *Principle Sources for British Research, pre-1837,* and the second is *Principle Sources for British Research, post-1837.* (Note – if you search for these videos by title, be sure to misspell the first word in the title – *Principle*, instead of using the word they should have used: *Principal*.) Each video is around thirty minutes. At the time of this writing, they were two of 154 video courses on doing British research (some were focused solely on British research, while others contained references to British research in videos about research in other countries). These courses can be found from the home page of *FamilySearch.org* by clicking on *Search*, and then on the next page click on *Wiki*. At the time of this writing, there were about 300 million names in FamilySearch's various British collections. So this would be a pretty good place to go when searching for your British ancestors.

The FamilySearch.org collection includes:

- English births and christenings, 1538 to 1975
- British deaths and burials, 1538 to 1991
- British marriages, 1538 to 1973

Society of Genealogists Library — *www.sog.org.uk*. I ran across this site when researching British records at FamilySearch.org. FamilySearch has partnered with SOG to show the images of a number of British records collections currently held by the LDS Church. It is a subscription website, but the subscription isn't too bad — £10.00 one-time charge plus £29.95 for one year's membership. That allows you online access to their records, plus free access to the library in London should you venture to London to do research there.

GENUKI

The GENUKI website (*www.genuki.org.uk/contents/*) is a genealogy site for the United Kingdom and Ireland. This is a great website to begin your research in England and / or Ireland. It's well organized, easy to understand and serves as a gateway to a large number of records. And – it's free, although some of the pages lead you to subscription or pay-per-view services.

National Archives — *discovery.nationalarchives.gov.uk/SearchUI/Home/ OnlineCollections*. If you're doing research on your British ancestors, you'll probably want to stop in at the British National Archives site. Like so many of the other sites for British genealogy, this site requires a pay-per-view fee to be able to see their records.

British Boys' First Names

Note – since you are reading this in English, you'll most likely recognize many English names on certificates. Below are a number of English names that have…gone out of style, for the most part, with which you may not be as familiar. Even though you may recognize some names, old English script is difficult to read, so these may assist you in deciphering the names you come across on various documents.

Aberle	Coburn
Alcott	Cromwell
Aldwyn	Darnell
Alger	Denham
Alvin	Denley
Atherton	Eadric
Beowulf	Gamel
Bourne	Godric
Brenton	Halvor
Bretton	Hamund
Bristol	Kirkley
Burl	Langham
Calhoun	Leighton
Cenwig	Peyton
Chadrick	Radcliff
Clive	Sheffield
	Thorn

> For much greater detail on researching my British or Scottish roots, check out Quillen's *Tracing Your Irish & British Roots*.

British Girls' First Names

Abelena	Fleta	Swete
Anice	Gunilda	Utta
Batilda	Gytha	Wynnfrith
Ceola	Heloise	Zelda
Cwenhild	Kinsey	
Deorwyn	Linsey	
Edith	Loveday	
Elfreda	Marlow	
Elvina	Mercia	
Ethelburh	Selda	

6. YOUR CZECH & SLOVAK ROOTS

The world stage continues to change. You may or may not be aware that in 1991, Czechoslovakia became two countries – the Czech Republic and Slovakia. So if you are researching your ancestral beginnings that lead back to that part of the world, you will have to deal with these two governmental entities. Needless to say, the fact that these two countries were part of the former Soviet Bloc poses additional research issues. But we'll give it a shot and direct you to those records that may be available.

Because your Czechoslovakian ancestors' records will likely be in two different countries, I'll share research information for both of those countries in this section.

The good news is that many Czech and Slovak records are being digitized, and as each day goes by (it seems) new records come online.

Key Records
There are a number of key records available as you begin your search for your British roots. Following are some of those sources:

Civil Registration
There are not many civil records available in the Czech Republic or Slovakia. The LDS Church was able to microfilm a few communities, generally near Germany. Those community records are available through *FamilySearch.org* on microfilm, either at their Family History Library in Salt Lake City, or by requesting them to be sent to a local Family History Center near you.

> Czechoslovakia
> now = Czech
> Republic and
> Slovakia

A few civil records are also available within various regions of the Czech Republic. Many of these (few) records have found their way online through the efforts of the various regional archival groups in the Czech Republic. And – good news – many of those records are online.

Church Records

The best records available are church records for Slovakia. There many church records there, and they were microfilmed by the LDS Church. These records are available through FamilySearch.org on microfilm, either at their Family History Library in Salt Lake City, or by requesting them to be sent to a local Family History Center near you. Some are available online through FamilySearch as well.

> Perhaps I should plan a *dovolená* in the Czech Republic ... (vacation!)

Helpful Websites for Czech Research
Following are websites that will be helpful as you venture into the Czech Republic in search of your ancestors:

FamilySearch.org – *www.familysearch.org* has a number of documents and videos courses about Czech research, and all are available to the public for free. I found a couple of great video courses that were helpful in learning and understanding Czech research. They are located at *https://familysearch.org/learningcenter/results.html?q=czech*.

In addition, FamilySearch.org has a respectable collection of Czech records and a few Slovak records, including:

• Czech births and baptisms, 1637 to 1889
• Czech censuses, 1843 to 1921
• Czech Church books 1552 to 1935
• Czech land records, 1450 to 1850
• Czech marriages, 1654 to 1889
• Czech nobility seigniorial records, 1619 to 1859
• Slovak church and synagogue books, 1592 to 1910

Many of the records are transcribed / abstracts, and many are digitized photos of the actual records. Generally I prefer the latter…but in the case of ancient records in Czech, Slovak, Russian, German or even Latin, I would be very happy to have an abstract or transcription!

Czech websites — Many of the records in the Czech Republic have been put online (good deal for genealogists!). However, before you get really excited, some of the websites (as of this writing) are not translated into English. In the top right-hand corner is typically a *Translate* icon, but many of these websites were only translated into French and German. So – if your German or French is better than your Czech, you're in luck! However, if you have been paying attention, you know that there are several translation sites on the Internet you can use to assist. Google Translate (*translate.google.com*) is good, as is *www.freetranslation.com*. You can copy and paste information from the page (in Czech, French or German) into one of those translation sites and usually get a pretty decent translation, at least enough for you to follow.

actapublica.eu/userdata/matriky_na_internetu_cr.pdf — this website provides a graphic representation of the areas for which the following websites have placed their records online.

www.actapublica.eu – this website gives you the opportunity to review parish records from the western-most regions of the Czech Republic. (Czech, German or French).

matriky.soalitomerice.cz/matriky_lite/ — this website covers the northwest portion of the Czech Republic – the area also known as Bohemia. This website is translated into English, which makes it a lot easier to navigate (for me, anyway!). The government hoped to have all of these records digitized and placed online by the end of 2012. Scanning the *Introduction: Inventory of Vital Records for Northern Bohemia* (which is in Czech), they have the parish records of the Catholic Church for some communities from 1558 to the 1900s.

www.ahmp.cz – this is a great website with a ton of genealogical information. Much of it is of ancient date, and covers the areas in and around Praha

(Prague – if you are doing Czech research, get used to the Czech name for Prague!). Alas, this website is only translated into Czech and German, making the navigation a little more difficult. If my Czech isn't failing me (nor the translation website I used!), they have put over 430,000 records on their website reaching back to the 1700s. The actual documents are located in the Prague City Hall.

Another great website that will lead you to valuable Czech genealogical websites is that of the Consulate General of the Czech Republic to New York: *www.mzv.cz/consulate.newyork/en/visa_and_consular_information/ancestors_in_the_czech_republic/index.html*.

www.vychodoceskearchivy.cz/zamrsk/ – this website covers the area directly to the east of Prague. They have digitized and made available to download over 3,300 parish registers from the eastern portion of the Czech Republic. This site is in Czech or translatable to German.

www.matriky.archives.cz/matriky_lite/ — this website covers the area of eastern Czech Republic. They boast records from the second half of the 16th century to the 20th century for the north Moravian region of the country. Their collection also contains civil records beginning in 1874. When you search the site, there will be a list of the various records they have. Once you select a record collection to review, you'll see an introduction to the collection – the years and places it covers, and the type of information (marriage, death, birth, etc.). Click on the digital photo of the record book (on the right center of the page, typically), and you'll be taken to the digitized document. The site is translated into English (or German, if you prefer!).

www. digi.ceskearchivy.cz/ — this website covers the region southwest of Prague. They have digitized a number of documents, including nobility seigniorial registers. It is translated into English, French and German.

Archives – there are archival sites located around the country. The previous section provides you with information about each of their websites, how to access them and a little about the records that are available there.

If you are unable to locate (or translate / figure out!) the information you are seeking on your ancestors, you may want to send a letter to one or more of the regional archives centers. Following is the English translation of a simple request for information on an ancestor. It is followed by translations in Czech and Slovak. Each of the regional websites includes a contact address (look for the *Kontakty* tab). If those efforts fail, you may wish to send them to the national archives location for the Czech Republic and Slovakia. Those addresses are included at the end of the translated letters.

June 15, 2013

Good day,

I live in the United States. My ancestors are from the Czech Republic (or Slovakia – depending on which country you are using). I would like to learn about them.

These are my ancestors who were born in the Czech Republic. Here is the information I have about them:

Last name:

First Name:

Date of birth (approximate):

Place of birth:

Father's given name and surname:

Mother's given name and surname: unknown

I request complete transcriptions of the original records.

Please tell me the cost of these services. The most I want to pay is $_____. If you send me a bill for the genealogy research, I will pay it. I understand you will not send the information until after I pay.

My address is:

(Enter your mailing address here)

Thank you,

Daniel Quillen
wdanielquillen@gmail.com

Here it is in Czech:

15 Červen 2013

Dobrý den,

Bydlím ve Spojených státech. Moji předkové pocházeli z České republiky. Rád bych o nich něco dozvědět.

Tyto jsou moji předkové who byly Narodil se v České republice. Tady je ta informace mám o ně.

Příjmení:

Název:

Místo narození:

Jméno otce:

Jméno matky za svobodna: neznámý

Žádám doslovné opisy záznamů s udáním použitých pramenů.

Prosím, řekněte mi náklady na tyto services. The nejvíce chci platit je $ _____. Pokud pošlete mi účet za genealogického výzkumu, budu platit. Chápu, nemusíte posílat informace až poté, co zaplatím.

Moje Adresa:

Děkuji,

Daniel Quillen wdanielquillen@gmail.com

And here it is in Slovak:

15 Jún, 2013

Dobrý deň,

Bývam v Spojených štátoch. Moji predkovia sú zo Slovenska. Rád by som sa o nich Žiadam o genealogických informácií o tejto osobe.

To sú moji predkovia, ktorí sa narodili na slovenskom. Tu je informácia, mám o nich:

Priezvisko:

Krstné meno:

Dátum narodenia (približne):

Miesto narodenia:

Meno otca:

Meno matky: nie je známe

Žiadam o kompletné prepisy z originálnych záznamov.

Prosím, povedzte mi náklady na tieto služby.

Moja adresa je:

(Enter your mailing address here)

D'akujem,

Daniel Quillen
wdanielquillen@gmail.com

For records older than 1951, letters such as the above should be sent to the following addresses:

Czech Republic
Archivní správa
Ministerstva vnitra CR
Milady Horákové 133
166 21 Praha 6
Czech Republic

Slovakia
Ministerstvo vnútra SR
Odbor archivníctva a spisovej slı
Križkova 7
811 04 Bratislava
Slovak Republic

Be sure and include as much information about the person for whose records you are searching. FamilySearch.org has a great document online that assists with your writing requests. It is found at *www.familysearch.org/ learn/wiki/en/images/b/bf/LWGCzechSlo.pdf*, and includes standard forms in English and Slovak with checkboxes for you to indicate the information you are seeking. That may be easier than trying to craft your own letters!

If you are seeking records for ancestors whose event (birth, death, marriage) occurred in Czechoslovakia's two largest cities – Prague (Praha) and Bratislava, you will most likely need to identify the section / parish of the city you want records from.

Be certain to tell them the most you are willing to pay for their services (see above). As of this writing, the Czech Republic does not use the euro. The Czech currency is the Czech crown (koruna), and the conversion rate is: $1

TRACING YOUR EUROPEAN ROOTS

dollar = 18 Czech crowns (so $100 would be roughly equal to 1,800 Czech crowns). In Slovakia, they do use the euro, so the conversion rate (as of this writing) is $1 = .76 euro, (so $100 would be roughly equal to 76 euro).

Be aware that requests may take up to six months to complete. So – hurry and get those requests in!

Slova, slova, slova / Slová, slová, slová (Words, words, words)

Below are words you are likely to run into as you research Czech records.

Czech:
babička – grandmother
brat – brother
civilně – civil
dátum narodenia – birth date
dcěra – daughter
dedko – grandfather
deň – day
dieťa – child
farský – parish
Jméno – given name
jméno matky za svobodna – mother's maiden name
Jméno za svobodna – maiden name
kmotr – godfather
kmotra – godmother
kněz – priest
křtěná – baptized
luteránský – Lutheran
manželství – marriage
měsíc – month
město – city
místo narození – birth place
muž – husband
náboženství – religion
narodil se / narodila se – he / she was born
narozený – born
názvem – name

osvědčení – certificate
pokřtěn – baptized
příjmení – last name, surname
římský katolík – Roman Catholic
rok – year
s názvem – named
sestra – sister
sto – hundred
strýc – uncle
syn – son
teta – aunt
tisíc – thousand
úmrtní list – death certificate
věk – age
žena / ženy – wife
ženatý – married
zemřel – died
zesnulý – deceased / died
židovský – Jewish

Slovak:
babička – grandmother
bratr – brother
civilní – civil
datum narození – birth date
dcera – daughter
dědeček – grandfather
den – day
dievčenské meno – maiden name
dítě – child
farní – parish
kmotra – godmother
kněz – priest
krstné meno – given name
krstný otec – godfather
luteránsky – Lutheran
manžel – husband
manželstvo – marriage
matka je rodné meno – mother's maiden name
mesiac – month
mesto – city

miesto narodenia – birth place
náboženstvo – religion
sa narodil / sa narodila – he / she was born
narodený – born
meno – name
osvedčenie – certificate
pokrstený – baptized
priezvisko – last name, surname
rímsky katolík – Roman Catholic
rok – year
s názvom – named
sestra – sister
sto – hundred
strýko – uncle
syn – son
teta – aunt
tisíc – thousand
úmrtný list – death certificate
věk – age
žena / ženy – wife
ženatý – married
židovský – Jewish
zomrel – died
zosnulý – deceased / died

Měsíce roku / Mesiace roka (*Months of the Year*)

Czech
> Leden – January
> Únor – February
> Březen – March
> Duben – April
> Květen – May
> Červen – June
> Červenec – July
> Srpen – August
> Září – September
> Říjen – October
> Listopadu – November
> Prosince – December

Slovak

Január – January
Február – February
Marec – March
Apríl – April
Máj – May
Jún – June
Júl – July
August – August
Septembra – September
Október – October
November – November
December – December

Names

Below are first names you are likely to run into as you are researching your Czech and Slovak ancestors. I have found that at least being familiar with the spelling of common names has helped me decipher many genealogy records through the years.

České a slovenské kluky jména (*Czech & Slovak boys first names*)

Adam
Aleksandr
Antonin
Aleš
Alexej
Andrej
Bedřich
Blažej
Bořivoj
Cenek
Dalibor
Dalimil
Drahomír
Drahoslav
Evžen
Honza
Ignác
Jan

Janek
Jiří
Josef
Karel
Kajetán
Kamil
Kazimír
Ladislav
Libor
Lubomír
Luboš
Miroslav
Pavel
Petr
Tadeáš

České a slovenské dívky jména (*Czech & Slovak girls first names*)

Alena
Alžběta
Amálie
Anastazie
Běla
Benedikta
Blanka
Bohumila
Bohuslava
Danica
Darina
Darja
Dorota
Eliška
Františka
Gabriela
Hedvika
Irenka
Iva
Ivana
Jana
Janička

Janička
Jiřína
Jitka
Kája
Katka
Lenka
Libuše
Livie
Taťána
Tereza
Vanda
Vlasta

7. YOUR FRENCH ROOTS

In the 2010 US census of the United States, nearly nine and a half million Americans indicated they were of French descent.

In recent years, the French government has made decisions that have delighted genealogists the world over – they have chosen to digitize and make available online many of the country's church, historical and government records. Read on and we'll discuss some of them.

One thing to bear in mind is that most of the records are kept at the town or *department* level in France. Departments are governmental units roughly equivalent to US counties. It would be well to know what department of France your ancestors came from, to allow you to narrow your search. There is a plethora of French genealogical records available for researchers, and it may be overwhelming if you do not know at least a general area of France from which your ancestor hailed.

Key Records
There are a number of key records available as you begin your search for your French roots. Following are some of those sources:

Civil Registration — Departments
France is divided into 100 departments, (four of which are overseas departments). During the Napoleonic period, the number of departments ranged from 83 to 130. While most records are kept at the town level, you need to discover in which department the town is situated.

As you peruse French websites and other sources, keep an eye out for records called Dicennial Tables Vital (*Tables décennales de l'état civil*). These tables list all births, deaths and marriages for each French *department* for a period of years. Most of the departments have at least several hundred years' worth of records. The information is arranged alphabetically by surname. Some great records are available at France GenWeb (*http://archives.cg08.fr/ arkotheque/tables_decennales/index.php*).

Censuses

If you have done much research in the United States, you know censuses can be a great tool for genealogists. While censuses in France predate those kept in the United States, they were not as uniformly administered, nor did they yield the same information.

The first French census was enumerated in 1772. The censuses between 1795 and 1836 do not include personal names. Censuses were taken every five years in France between 1836 to 1936. There is no census for 1916 – the French were pretty busy trying not to have to learn German.

French law requires a 100-year waiting period for reviewing census records, but several sources I have read indicate that some archivists will allow censuses as recent as thirty or forty years to be reviewed. Since the national censuses are kept at the department level, it really does appear to be at the whim of the local archivist as to whether viewing will be allowed.

Since 1836, French censuses gathered first and surnames, age, occupation, nationality and often place of birth.

If you know your ancestor lived in a particular town or area in France, you might give this a try. French census records have not been indexed, so you'll have to peruse them page-by-page.

At the time of this writing, FamilySearch had not microfilmed nor put online French census records. However, I have had some luck finding French census records by Googling *France (name of department) (name of town) census*. Some of the departments have digitized their censuses and put them online, while many have not.

Parish Records

Prior to the requirement for civil registration, France did as many of her neighbors did: required clergy to keep keen records of all births, deaths and marriages. Consequently, these records are pretty extensive and a great find for genealogists. Civil registration began in 1792, but before (and after) that, clergy kept great records. Many of those church records – some extending back to the mid-1500s – are available online.

Parish death records were kept by most clergy from 1539 on, and they generally included at least the age of the individual who had died, and on occasion his or her birth date. The government required this information to be copied and provided to them, so these records are often available online or through microfilm.

Thank goodness for the Catholic Church's record-keeping policies!

Marriage records almost always included the bride's and groom's names as well as their ages. Occasionally, their birth or christening dates were also included.

Wills & Probate Records

Like many western European countries, France has a long history of and a large number of wills and probate records. These records seldom included birth dates, but most often included death dates. As with many of the French records, wills and other probate records are housed at the department level.

Wills and probate records will likely provide the names of the individual's spouse (no mention of him or her may indicate they pre-deceased the individual), and children may be listed also. These documents also provide a peek into your ancestors' lives, as you see the extent of their wealth (or lack thereof), and the things they will to their heirs. Through the years, I have seen such items as "my favorite pewter cup, four sheep, my willow chair," etc. willed to heirs.

Helpful Websites for French Research

Following are websites that will be helpful as you search for your French ancestors:

France GenWeb Wiki — *www.francegenweb.org/~wiki/index.php/Accueil* — you should bookmark this site, as it will be a marvelous gateway into the world of online French records. Church records, government records and historical records will all vie for your attention. When you arrive at the site, it is written in French, but just click the translation button and you can translate it into one of many languages, including English.

As of this writing, the way to find their online records is to look in the *Archives* box on the first page, and then *Map of France Archives Online*. That will take you to a color-coded map of the country, which will tell you which archives are online for each department. The vast majority have at least some records online, and only a very few departments have no records online. The color-coded map lets you know which departments have records and in what format.

At the bottom of the map, they even show you which of their colonies / protectorates have records online (St. Martin, Guadalupe, New Caledonia, etc.).

Just poke around on the site until you find the records collection you are seeking. This is one of the better websites out there for international research.

Ancestry.com
Ancestry.com's international subscription edition contains an extensive French section, including nearly 150 records collections. Included among their collections are some of the following:

• Paris & vicinity marriage banns 1860 to 1902
• Upper Brittany marriages, 1536 to 1907
• Alsace-Lorraine citizenship declarations, 1872
• Marne births, 1501 to 1907
• Marne marriages 1529 to 1907
• Paris and vicinity births 1700 to 1899
• Paris death notices 1860 to 1902

If you are doing a lot of genealogical research in France, it may well be worth the money to get an Ancestry.com subscription for a few months. Their collections cover the critical events of millions of French individuals.

You can find a list of all Ancestry.com's French collections by going to *search.ancestry.com/search/CardCatalog.aspx#ccat=hc%3D25%26dbSort%3D1%26title%3DFrance%26keyword%3D%26.*

Cyndi's List – *www.cyndislist.com* – Cyndi's List remains a favorite genealogical site for me, and her links to French records are extensive. What's more, they included links that I haven't found other places. She's saved you the effort of Googling various records.

FamilySearch.org – *www.familysearch.org* has a number of documents and video courses about French research, and all are available to the public for free.

FamilySearch.org has a nice collection of French records, among them:

• France Births and Baptisms, 1546 to 1895
• France Deaths and Burials, 1546 to 1960
• France Marriages, 1546 to 1924
• France, Coutances Catholic Diocese, 1802 to 1907
• France, Protestant Church Records, 1612 to 1906
• France, Quimper et Léon Catholic Diocese, 1772 to 1909

These collections contain the names and information on about nine million individuals.

French National Archives — *http://www.archivesnationales.culture.gouv.fr/arn/.* If you're doing research on your French ancestors, you'll probably want to stop in at the French National Archives (*Archives Nationales*) site. It's a nice place to get a feel of the records available in their national archives. While most French records of interest to genealogists are kept at the department level, there are still some records held nationally that may be of interest. A caution about this website – it is in French (naturally!), but like so many of these international websites, has a *Translate* icon.

Vienne parish registers — *www.archives-vienne.cg86.fr/639-les-registres-paroissiaux.htm* — I include this website as an example of the websites maintained by many of the departments in France. Vienne is a small department in west-central France, and has put their parish records online for genealogists to explore. Their website includes images of parish registers, censuses, land records, various church records, etc.

Drop-down boxes allow you to select the area for your research, the institution or type of record (for example: marriage records held at the Notre Dame Catholic Church in Beaumont, Vienne department).

Even if you don't have ancestors in this part of France, this is a good website to give a whirl, to familiarize yourself with what you can expect from many of the departments.

If all your efforts fail at uncovering online or microfilm documents for your ancestors, you may consider writing a letter. Following is a sample letter in English, with the French translation following:

June 15, 2013

Good day,

I live in the United States. My ancestors are from France. I would like to learn about them.

Here is the information I have about my ancestors that were born in France:

Last name:

First Name:

Date of birth (approximate):

Place of birth:

Father's given name and surname:

Mother's given name and surname: unknown
I request complete transcriptions of the original records.

Please tell me the cost of these services. The most I want to pay is
US$_____. If you send me a bill for the genealogy research, I will
pay it. I understand you will not send the information until after I pay.

My address is:
(Enter your mailing address here)

Thank you,

Daniel Quillen
wdanielquillen@gmail.com

And here's the same letter in French:

15 Juin 2013

Bonne journée,

Je vis aux États-Unis. Mes ancêtres sont de France. Je voudrais
apprendre à leur sujet.

Voici les informations que j'ai sur mes ancêtres qui sont nés en France:

Nom de famille:

Prénom:

Date de naissance (approximative):

Lieu de naissance:

Nom donné du père et prénom:

Prénom de la mère et le prénom: inconnu

Je demande complète des transcriptions des documents originaux.

S'il vous plaît dites-moi le coût de ces services. Le plus je tiens à rendre aux États-Unis est $_____. Si vous m'envoyez un projet de loi pour la recherche généalogique, je vais le payer. Je comprends que vous ne vous enverrons de l'information jusqu'à ce que je payer.

Mon adresse est:
(Enter your mailing address here)

Je vous remercie,

Daniel Quillen
wdanielquillen@gmail.com

Des mots, des mots, des mots (*Words, words, words*)
Below are words you are likely to run into as you research French records.

acte – certificate, record
act de décés – death certificate
adulte – adult
âge – age
an / année – year
arrondissement – district / ward
baptême – baptism
cent – hundred
civile – civil
con – to
décédé / décés / défunt – deceased
dénomé – named
des or du – from

epouse – wife
epoux – husband
est née / est né – was born (feminine / masculine)
femme – wife / woman
feu / feue – late, deceased
fille – daughter
fils – son
frère – brother
grand-mère – grandmother
grand-père — grandfather
jour – day
mari—husband
marriage — marriage
marié – married
marraine — Godmother
mere — mother
mil / mille – thousand
mois – month
mort – died
naissance – birth
né / née – born (also maiden name)
nom – name
oncle — uncle
Parrain – Godfather
père — father
prêtre – priest / minister / pastor
soeur — sister
tante — aunt

Mois de l'année *(Months of the year)*
Janvier — January
Février — February
Mars — March
Avril – April
Mai — May
Juin — June
Juillet — July

Août — August
Setembre — September
Octobre — October
Novembre – November
Décembre – December

Names

Below are first names you are likely to run into as you are researching your French ancestors. I have found that at least being familiar with the spelling of common names has helped me decipher many genealogy records through the years.

Prénoms français masculins *(French boys given names)*
Alexandre
Alphonse
Amaury
André
Antoine
Arnaud
Edouard
Etienne
Francois
Frédéric
Gaston
Georges
Gérard
Grégoire
Guillaume
Henri
Jacques
Jean
Julien
Luc
Lucien
Mathieu
Michel

Nicolas
Philippe
Pierre
Raoul
René
Thibaut
Thierry
Tristan
Xavier
Yves

Les jeunes filles françaises des noms *(French girls given names)*
Adele
Agathe
Amélie
Anastasie
Andrée
Antoinette
Arnaude
Astrid
Aurélie
Aurore
Brigitte
Capucine
Catherine
Cécile
Céline
Claire
Claudine
Corinne
Danielle
Dorothée
Eléonore
Francoise
Frédérique
Gabriele

Geneviéve
Héléne
Laetitia
Luce
Martine
Monique
Noémi
Pénélope
Renée
Simone
Thérése
Virginie
Zoe

8. YOUR GERMAN ROOTS

Willkommen! If your genealogical roots return to Germany, you are in good company: according to the 2010 US Census, more than 50 million Americans said they were of German ancestry – that's nearly one in six Americans. My wife – maiden name Blau – and I both have German ancestors.

There is good news and bad news when it comes to researching your German ancestors. On the one hand, the quest for German records is aided and abetted by the legendary work ethic and organizational skills of the German people. On the other hand, you are also unfortunately handicapped by distance and the fact that two disastrous World Wars were fought on and over German soil. Many genealogical records were destroyed; fortunately, many also survived. But – if you know where to look you'll be able to locate many genealogical records of the German people.

German records are often kept at the village (*dorf*), city (*stadt*), county (*kreis / bezirk*) or state (*staat*) levels. Knowing something of Germany and its geographical structures is helpful. Germany is made up of many former and ancient kingdoms, provinces and duchies. Many of the records that were created are kept in the equivalent of the county seat of these various entities. There are sixteen states in Germany, and each state is divided into counties.

German States
- Baden-Württemberg
- Bavaria (*Bayern*)
- Berlin
- Brandenburg
- Bremen (*Freie Hansestadt Bremen*)
- Hamburg
- Hessen

- Lower Saxony (*Niedersachsen*)
- Mecklenburg–Vorpommern
- North Rhine Westphalia (*Nordrhein Westfalen*)
- Rhineland Palatinate (*Rheinland-Pfalz*)
- Saarland
- Saxony (*Sachsen*)
- Saxony Anhalt (*Sachsen-Anhalt*)
- Schleswig-Holstein
- Thuringia (*Thüringen*)

Watch for these places when you are doing your research. While many may look foreign to you the first time or two that you see them, they may hold important genealogical keys.

One of the most important pieces of information for you to find while doing German research is the place where your ancestors came from. Once you identify the town, you can find that town on a map of Germany. A good gazetteer of Germany may be necessary to assist you in pinpointing which county (*kreis*) the town is in, which in turn will indicate what state it is in.

German Patronymics
As with other European peoples, the Germans also had naming customs. Although not hard and fast, these naming customs can help you identify ancestors' names further up the family tree. For sons, it was often the custom to name each son in the following fashion:

First son – paternal grandfather's name
Second son – maternal grandmother's name
Third son – father's name
Fourth son – father's father's father's name
Fifth son – mother's father's father's name
Sixth son – father's mother's father's name
Seventh son – mother's mother's father's name

And daughters were often named after the following manner:

First daughter – maternal grandmother's name
Second daughter – paternal grandmother's name
Third daughter – mother's name
Fourth daughter – father's father's mother's name
Fifth daughter – mother's father's mother's name
Sixth daughter – father's mother's mother's name
Seventh daughter – mother's mother's mother's

I can understand and keep straight the first naming customs for the first three sons / daughters, but I don't know how anyone kept the next three straight! In fact, maybe some didn't, because there are several known naming patterns for Germans; all are the same for the first three children, but differ somewhat for the next three or four children.

Watch the middle names of my ancestors – they may provide clues to their grandparents' names!

Germans often selected two names for their children. The first, typically after a saint, was considered the individual's spiritual name, and the middle name was the name the child went by. For example, in Germany it was very common to give a son the spiritual name of Johann or George (often spelled Georg). So, Johann Friedrich Blau would often have been called Friedrich. Girls were also given a spiritual name: perhaps Johanna, Anna or Maria. So Johanna Hannelore Schmidt went by Hannelore Schmidt. An interesting side note on the spiritual name Johan / Johann: it is a name honoring Saint John. As a spiritual name, it was almost always spelled Johan or Johann. If used as a middle name, it was almost always spelled Johannes.

It is interesting to note that while the practice of providing a spiritual first name was originally associated with Catholicism, as Protestantism spread in Germany, the practice continued, even among Protestant families. Also, it was common for the same spiritual name to be given to all the children of the same gender in a family.

Immigration Center Applications

In Chapter Three, I mentioned using immigration records held by the United States government to find clues about your European ancestors. Germany also kept immigration records. These records are called *Einwanderungszentralstelle Anträge* — EWZ files, and they are chock full of genealogical information.

Between 1939 and 1945, Germany received over 400,000 applications for citizenship from individuals seeking naturalized German citizenship. Each claimed to be a German living outside of the country. These detailed records include names of the applicant, his or her spouse and children as well as the names of their parents and grandparents. They also provide dates and places of birth for each of those individuals – just what you are searching for; it's like a genealogist designed the form! Many of the applications have extensive documentation to support their German roots – letters detailing multiple generations of German ancestors, family trees, marriage and birth certificates, etc.

Information in the EWZ files are grouped first by the country or region where the applicant was living, and then alphabetically by surname thereafter.

EWZ files can be found in a variety of places, including:

- Purchase EWZ microfilm rolls from the National Archives (800-234-8861). They are available for $35.
- FamilySearch.org has all the EWZ files on microfilm. You can either check them out at the Family History Library in Salt Lake City or order them and view them at a Family History Center near your home.
- Personally go to the National Archives in the Washington DC area (College Park, MD).
- Tom Stangl is an EWZ researcher who lives in the Washington, DC area and will research files for you. He asks that you reimburse him for travel, copying and mailing costs. You can contact him at tstanglsr@aol.com.

As you would expect, EWZ files are in German. Also, most of the EWZ files I have reviewed are difficult to read because the images are not sharp.

Although most of the information in the files is typed, the combination of my poor German and the poor image quality makes it difficult to decipher the name of each section. If that's the case for you, this website provides an English translation of the EWZ form: *http://www.rollintl.com/roll/ewz.htm*. It is very helpful.

Many of the EWZ files are available through the LDS Church archives. The LDS church has microfilmed most of the EWZ records, and they are available to you through visits to their Family History Library or any of the many local Family History Centers.

Once you have located an ancestor in the EWZ files, you will also want to search the Stammblätter – family group sheets or pedigree charts. More information will likely be found there. To use the Stammblätter, look up the name of the person in the card index (E/G Kartei) to obtain the case number, then locate the case number in the record for the "*Stammblätter*" to obtain the film number.

Emigration Records
In addition to *immigration* records, Germany kept *emigration* records – records of those leaving Germany for other locations. There is a set of emigration records that captured critical information about emigrants who left Germany's shores for other lands between 1850 and 1934. (Few records were kept during the years of World War I, 1915 – 1919.) Most German emigration records were destroyed during World War II, but the emigrations records for the port of Hamburg survived intact. They are referred to as the **Hamburg Passenger Lists**. The 5,000,000 records were predominantly German, although over 1,000,000 of the records are for emigrants from other European countries, such as Poland, Russia, Sweden, Finland, Norway and Denmark. Each entry typically includes the name, date of birth and date of departure for each emigrant and for many, their town of birth or residence – great information for genealogists. Later passenger lists included additional information, such as relation to head of household (the person leading the emigrating party).

According to the research I have done, those traveling out of Hamburg were typically coming from northeastern Germany, the Scandinavian countries and Russia. Those traveling from northwestern Germany typically left out of Bremen. There are very few 19th-century records for those who traveled from Bremen, but there are records of 20th-century travelers. Those coming from southern Germany (Bavaria) often took a train to Le Havre, France. Unfortunately there are no records for those departing from Le Havre.

All that said, even if my ancestors hailed from northwestern or southern Germany or one of the other countries that typically sailed out of Bremen or Le Havre, I would still search the Hamburg passenger lists.

Let's focus on the Hamburg passenger lists. There are two types of Hamburg passenger lists:

1. **Direct passenger lists** refer to the lists of those who left Hamburg and sailed directly to their destinations without transfers to other trans-oceanic ships at other European ports. The lists for 1850 to 1855 are not complete, but do contain information that may be of assistance. The 1850 to 1855 lists are arranged alphabetically by the first letter of the surname of the person identified as the head of household. After 1855, the lists are arranged chronologically based on when ships left Hamburg port.

2. **Indirect passenger lists** are the lists of those who sailed from Hamburg and transferred to other ships before sailing for their final destination. The indirect lists are for the period 1854 to 1910; individuals who left before 1854 or after 1910 are included in the Direct passenger lists.

"Why," you ask, "would someone take an indirect route rather than a direct route to America?" Often the answer was the same as it is today: cost. If I fire up Orbitz and look for a flight, sometimes I can get cheaper fares by taking a flight the makes one or two stops enroute to my ultimate destination. Such was also the case in the late 19th and early 20th centuries with ship travel. Fares from Hamburg directly to America were frequently more expensive than fares from other ports – Le Havre, or Liverpool, for example. Many with large families chose the indirect routes rather than pay the extra fare for a direct passage.

If you don't want to subscribe to Ancestry.com, or can't get to someplace that has a subscription that you can use (like your local library, perhaps), the LDS Church is another place to find the Hamburg passenger lists. They have nearly 500 rolls of microfilm containing the passenger lists, and they are available to view by either going to the main Family History Library in Salt Lake City, or by renting them for a nominal fee and having them sent to one of their thousands of local Family History Centers around the world. (Note, however, that Hamburg State Archives of Germany do not allow the rolls to be sent to a Family History Center in Germany. In Germany, the records must be viewed at a Hamburg State Archives location.)

Clan Books

Another wonderful source of information for German research are *Ortsippenbucher* – Clan books. Clan books are sort of like family histories of entire German towns or villages. If you are able to identify the town or area your ancestor came from, discovery of an *Ortsippenbuch* for that area may yield several generations of genealogical (and other) information about them. The information in the books is gleaned from church records, civil registries, etc., and includes birth, death, marriage and other records.

A good website about Ortsippenbuch is found at *www.feefhs.org/igs/ igsorts.html*, a website maintained by the **Federation of East European Family History Societies**. It lists all the towns and cities, by state, which have Ortsippenbuchs available. To get the most information from these books, you must know the place where your ancestor came from. Virtually all the Ortsippenbucher are in German.

If you are stymied by the German you find in any of these documents, there are a number of fine on-line German-to-English dictionaries available. Two websites I have used extensively are *www.freetranslations.com* and *dict.tu- chemnitz.de* (note: no *www.* is required on the second website). Google Translate (*www.translate.google*) is a great translation website also.

These few websites just scratch the surface of the information available for German genealogical work. Cyndi'sList (*www.cyndislist.com*) alone lists over 216 German-specific websites for doing genealogy.

If all your efforts fail at uncovering online or microfilm documents for your ancestors, you may consider writing a letter. Following is a sample letter in English, with the German translation following:

June 15, 2013

Good day,

I live in the United States. My ancestors are from Germany. I would like to learn about them.

Here is the information I have about my ancestors that were born in Germany:

Last name:

First Name:

Date of birth (approximate):

Place of birth:

Father's given name and surname:

Mother's given name and surname: unknown

I request complete transcriptions of the original records. Please tell me the cost of these services. The most I want to pay is US$_____. If you send me a bill for the genealogy research, I will pay it. I understand you will not send the information until after I pay.

My address is:
(Enter your mailing address here)

Thank you,

Daniel Quillen
wdanielquillen@gmail.com

And here it is in German:

15 Juni 2013

Guten Tag,

Ich lebe in den Vereinigten Staaten. Meine vorfahren stammen aus der Deutschland. Ich möchte über sie zu erfahren.

Hier sind die informationen habe ich über meine vorfahren, die in Deutschland geboren wurden:

Nachname:

Vorname:

Geburtsdatum (ca.):

Geburtsort:

Vaters Vor-und Nachname:
Mutter-und nachname: unbekannt

Ich bitte vervollständigen transkriptionen der originaldaten.

Bitte sagen sie mir die kosten für diese dienstleistungen. Das möchte ich zahlen ist US $ _____. Wenn sie mir eine rechnung für die ahnenforschung, werde ich es bezahlen. Ich verstehe Sie nicht senden Sie die Informationen erst, nachdem ich bezahlen.

Meine adresse ist:
(Enter your address here)

Vielen dank,

Daniel Quillen
wdanielquillen@gmail.com

Worte, Worte, Worte *(Words, words, words)*
Below are words you are likely to run into as you research German records.

ausgewandert – emigrated (don't you just love that one? Literally "out traveled" or "out wandered!").
bestätigung — confirmation
bestätigen — confirmed
ehe — marriage
ehemann — husband
eltern — parents
enkel — grandson
enkelin — granddaughter
frau/ehefrau — wife
geburt — birth
gemeinde — parish
gescheiden — divorced
großmutter — grandmother
großvater — grandfather
hausmutter – mother of the house
hausvater – father of the house
Im jahre des heils – in the year of our Lord (note: heils means salvation)
jahre — year
Katholik — Catholic
kind/kinder — child/children
kirche — church
kreis — county
ledig (abbreviated as *led.*) — single
Lutherische — Lutheran
monat — month
mutter — mother
onkel — uncle
pfarre: parsonage / vicarage / parish
schwester — sister
sohn — son
tag – day
tante — aunt

taufe/getauft — baptism/baptized
tochter — daughter
verheiratet (abbreviated as *verh.*) — married
verwitwet (abbreviated as *verw.*) — widowed
vater — father
vergraben — buried
witwe — widow
witwer — widower
zensus — census

Monaten des Jahres *(Months of the year)*
Januar — January
Februar — February
Marz — March
Abril — April
Mai — May
Juni — June
Juli — July
August — August
September — September
Oktober — October
November — November
Dezember – December

Names
Below are first names you are likely to run into as you are researching your German ancestors. I have found that at least being familiar with the spelling of common names has helped me decipher many genealogy records through the years.

Deutsch Jungen Vornamen *(German boys first names)*
Albrecht
Andreas
Axel
Bernhard
Bruno

Dieter
Dominik
Ernst
Franz
Friedrich
Georg
Gerhard
Gottfried
Günther
Heinrich
Jakob
Johann
Josef
Karl
Klaus
Konrad
Ludwig
Matthias
Peter
Rudolf
Siegfried
Steffen
Torsten
Ulrivh
Uwe
Viktor
Walter
Wilhelm

Deutsch Mädchen Vornamen *(Girls' Names)*
Anja
Anneliese
Beate
Beatrix
Berta
Brigitte

9. YOUR IRISH ROOTS

Inasmuch as this is a genealogy book written by an American of Irish descent, I had to put in a chapter on Irish genealogical research! Here are three interesting genealogical facts about Irish genealogy:

1. In the 2010 US census of the United States, nearly 37 million Americans considered themselves of Irish descent;

2. Another 43 million indicated that at least one of their progenitors was Irish;

3. Seventy percent of American travelers to Ireland each year say they have at least one Irish ancestor.

Doing Irish genealogical research can be enlightening and exhilarating. It can also be extremely frustrating. Once you leave the United States, headed back to the "ould country," you need to understand what records are available, and how to access those records.

But first – and by now you should know what I am going to say – learn all you can from your parents, grandparents, aunts, uncles, etc. From this perspective, Irish research is no different from any other ethnic research. Collect information, stories, certificates, etc. Perhaps your family has a tradition that great uncle Paddy worked on the Titanic as a welder, or that your second great grandfather lost all his family in the potato famine. Stories like these can provide clues that will help you locate your family.

Regardless of when your Irish ancestors left the Emerald Isle, your research gets more difficult once your family roots go back to her green shores for a number of reasons. First of all, you'll discover that generations of genealogical records were destroyed during the Civil War that erupted in Ireland in 1922, a tragic and lamentable fact. It ranks right up there with the burning of the 1890 US census as one of the saddest genealogical events for genealogists. This destruction of about 900 years of records makes searching for your Irish ancestors a little more difficult. But we'll forge ahead, and I'll show you some viable options for finding them.

For more details, check out Quillen's *Tracing Your Irish & British Roots*

Another reason for the scarcity of records was the fact that many simply weren't kept. Vital statistics that are a genealogist's best friend (birth, marriage, death records) weren't required by the Irish government until 1864. The Catholic Church, that great genealogical organization that kept records in all its parishes throughout the world for centuries, was forbidden by Ireland's conquerors (the British) from keeping records during most of the 18th century (although many did anyway!).

But don't despair…there is hope. The Church of Ireland kept records. Land deeds were kept of land transactions, wills were kept, and several censuses were taken. Passenger lists containing the names of thousands of Irish immigrants were kept. The Irish were very clannish, and often a clan lived in the same part of Ireland for many, many generations.

There are several books that will be of assistance in finding where your ancestors called home.

The first is *Irish Family Names* (W. W. Norton & Company, Inc., New York, NY 1989) by Brian de Breffny. Another is *The Surnames of Ireland* (Irish Academic Press Limited, 1999, Blackrock, Co. Dublin) by Edward MacLysaght. Both provide excellent listings of many Irish family names and their counties of origin. Another outstanding book on Irish families and their ancestral counties is *The Complete Book of Irish Family Names* (Irish Genealogical Foundation, 1989) by Michael C. O'Laughlin. (Note: The first two books listed here are out of print, but some used ones are still offered through Amazon.com.)

Let's talk about some topics and resources you should be aware of which will assist you in searching for your Irish ancestors.

Geographical Units

There are several governmental and antiquated jurisdictional units in Ireland that it would be well for you to know about. Not knowing one or more of them may cause you to run screaming into the night as you strive to make sense out of Irish records you find.

- **Townland** – this is a term I suspect you may not be familiar with. It is roughly equivalent to the township in American vernacular, but is generally much smaller. A townland may be as small as 300 to 400 acres. It could be a small town. As you look at older Irish records, you may well run into this term.
- **Parish** — A series of townlands together make up a parish.
- **Poor Law Union** – also known as a PLU, this is a term you have probably not heard, but if you do much work with Irish records, you are sure to run into. PLUs were jurisdictional areas that typically consisted of a number of parishes, and were considered civil registration districts. Older records in particular will contain the name of a PLU, rather than a parish or county name. Some of the PLUs in the country carry the names of Irish towns, lakes, etc. A typical PLU may consist of from twenty to forty parishes, and a county may be made up of from two to fifteen PLUs (most common is four or five). PLUs grew out of the workhouse system – a sort of unemployment assistance effort for areas that were particularly poor or struggling financially. If you go to *www.seanruad.com,* you can find what PLU your townland or parish was part of. Use this if you find a record that has a PLU listed on it.
- **County** – there are 26 counties in Ireland, and six in Northern Ireland. Prior to 1922, there were thirty-two counties. But in 1922, twenty-six of the Irish counties won independence from Great Britain. Six chose to stay with Great Britain, creating what we have today as Northern Ireland. If you have ancestors with an event (birth, death, marriage, etc.) prior to 1922, their records will show Ireland as their country.
- **Province** – while you don't hear much about provinces any longer, and there are no records kept at the province level, you may hear their names mentioned: Ulster, Leinster, Munster and Connacht.

It's good to keep these geographical juris-dictions in mind as you search for your ancestors' records. If you find a name of a jurisdictional unit that just doesn't add up, be sure and review the information above to see how it might fit.

PLU = Poor Law Union = Civil Registration District

Key Records

There are a number of key records available as you begin your search for your Irish roots. Following are some of those sources:

Censuses

Irish censuses were kept beginning in 1801, but the 1821, 1831, 1841 and 1851 censuses were almost entirely destroyed in 1922. The 1901 and 1911 censuses are now available to the public. The 1921 census won't be available until 2021, since like the British censuses, Irish censuses won't be released until 100 years have passed since the enumeration.

Civil Registration

Civil registration (the registering of births, marriages and deaths by the government) began in Ireland much later than most other western Euro-pean countries – 1864. Protestant marriages (primarily in the area now known as Northern Ireland) commenced in 1845.

In 1922 a nasty civil war erupted in Ireland over differences between the treaty with England that annexed six northern counties of Ulster to England – the area on the Emerald Isle known as Northern Ireland. The genealogical significance of this civil war is that during the fighting, approximately 900 years of Irish records were destroyed when one of the armies booby-trapped the Four Courts, a government building where those genealogy records were unfortunately stored. The booby-trap was tripped, and although no soldiers were killed, nearly a thousand years of Irish genealogical records were lost.

Since that time, the National Archives has been busy trying to cobble together records from other sources that were not destroyed – land records spread across the country, wills and probate records, etc.

However – all is not lost. Many civil registration records were kept within the Poor Law Union areas of the country. Many of those records have been extracted by FamilySearch and can be found in their databases, although most of the available information are abstracts and/or indexes.

In addition, copies of birth, marriage and death certificates can be gotten from the *General Register Office* in Roscommon, Ireland for the Republic, and the *General Register Office* for Northern Ireland in Belfast. For the Republic, send your request to:

> General Register Office
> Government Offices
> Convent Road
> Roscommon, Ireland

For specific information you can visit their website at *www.groireland.ie*. They are quick to point out they do not do genealogical research for you, but will either provide certified copies or photocopies of the birth, marriage or death registers.

And for the North, much of the information available there can be gotten online at the following website: *www.nidirect.gov.uk/index/research-your-family-history*. Fees are associated with requests and research, and the website does a pretty good job of identifying the costs of each type request you may have.

Be certain and provide as much information as you know about an individual to ensure that you receive information about the correct person.

Helpful Websites for Irish Research

Following are websites that will be helpful as you search for your Irish ancestors:

Ancestry.com

Ancestry.com's international subscription edition includes a list of over 100 records collections representing millions of Irish individuals. It includes the following:

- 1841 & 1851 Census extracts for Northern Ireland
- 1841 & 1851 Census extracts for the Republic of Ireland
- Famine relief commission papers, 1844 to 1847
- Tithe applotment books, 1823 to 1837
- 1851 census for County Antrim
- 1766 religious census

Ancestry Ireland – *www.ancestryireland.com*. Ancestry Ireland is the website for the Ulster Historical Foundation, and provides a great resource for genealogists seeking their Ulster ancestors. They have over two million records available online, including birth, marriage and death records for Counties Antrim and Down. They also have tombstone inscriptions and census records. They are a pay-per-view subscription service; credits cost £1 each. Viewing records costs from one to four credits, depending on the type record you view. You can purchase a Guild membership for £31 a year and the cost of viewing records is cut in half. So if you have Ulster ancestors from one of those counties and will be searching a number of records, the Guild membership may be the way to go for you.

FamilySearch.org – *www.familysearch.org* has a number of documents and video courses about Irish research, and all are available to the public for free. I found the following video course especially helpful in understanding Irish research: Irish Civil Registration (*broadcast.lds.org/elearning/FHD/Community/en/FamilySearch/IrelandBeginningResearch/Ireland_Civil_Registration/Player.html*). At the time of this writing, it was one of 145 video courses on doing Irish research. These courses can be found by clicking the *Search* tab on the *FamilySearch.org* home page, and then clicking on *Wiki* on the next page.

From the *Research Wiki* page, enter *Irish research* in the *Search* box, and you'll be treated to (as of this writing) over 750 articles on Irish research

In addition, FamilySearch.org has a very large collection of Irish records, including:

- Irish births and baptisms, 1620 to 1881
- Ireland deaths, 1864 to 1870

- Irish civil registration indexes, 1845 to 1958
- Irish marriages, 1619 to 1898

Those records collections above represent about 26 million Irish names.

Along with other miscellaneous records and family histories, the Family History Library in Salt Lake City has more than 3,000 books, over 11,500 microfilms and 3,000 microfiche containing information about the people of Ireland. Virtually all of these records are available to you no matter where you live by making a visit to a Family History Center at the local LDS chapel nearest where to you live.

GENUKI

The GENUKI website (*www.genuki.org.uk/contents/*) is a genealogy site for the United Kingdom and Ireland. This is a great website to begin your research in Ireland and / or England. It's well organized, easy to understand and serves as a gateway to a large number of records. And – it's free, although some of the pages lead you to subscription or pay-per-view services.

Irish Genealogy — *www.irishgenealogy.ie.* This is a great, free website that provides abstracts of a large number of Irish genealogy records. Baptism, birth, death and marriage records are all available. As of this writing, they have over 3 million pre-1900 records available to search. So far it is somewhat limited in scope – its records include church records of the Roman Catholic Church and the Church of Ireland from Counties Carlow, Cork, Kerry and Dublin City. But they are adding records all the time, and those digitized records are free to view online. The project is being funded by *Department of Arts, Heritage and the Gaeltacht* and through the work of the *Dublin Heritage Group* and *Kerry Genealogical Research Centre*. Let's hope they continue funding the project!

Irish Newspaper Archives – *www.irishnewsarchive.com.* This is a great site that allows access to hundreds of years of Irish newspapers – back to the 1700s. It is a subscription site, which allows you to browse to your heart's content for 24 hours (€10), 48 hours (€15), one week (€25), one month (€60) or one year (€350).

Irish Origins — *www.irishorigins.com*. This is one of the early entries into the Irish genealogy subscription services website race, and, like their British affiliate mentioned in Chapter 5, I really like them. They offer access to over 80 million records, including censuses, wills, birth, marriage and death certificates, burial and cemetery records, etc.

Unlike several of their European competitors (see *Roots Ireland* below) *Irish Origins* allows monthly and annual subscriptions. You can get a combined British and Irish subscription or if you're only interested in Irish genealogy, you can get an Ireland-only subscription. Costs as of this writing are:

	72-hour	Monthly	Annual
British only	£7.00	£9.50	(not available)
Irish only	£6.00	£9.50	(not available)
Combination	£8.00	£10.50	£55.00

Note these prices are in British pounds (£), not euros or dollars. As of this writing, the conversion rate is $1.60 per £1. So £7 = $11.20.

National Archives – *www.nationalarchives.ie/genealogy1*. Take a few minutes and check out the website for the Irish National Archives. Most of the records are only available via microfilm and paper to be viewed onsite, but in a great boon for genealogists, the 1901 and 1911 censuses are online and can be viewed – or at least abstracts of them can be viewed. While the abstract is first presented, you can click on an icon and you can see the actual census page. To see either census, go to *www.census.nationalarchives.ie/search*. And the price is definitely right – it's free!

Roots Ireland — *www.rootsireland.ie* is one of the newer websites focused on Irish genealogy. They boast over 18 million Irish genealogy records online, about half of them birth certificates. Roots Ireland is a subscription website. You purchase credits (the denomination is in euro, not dollars), and then you use your credits to view records. Searching is free, but if you want to view more than the index of a record, then you must pay with your credits. It is possible to purchase enough credits to see just one record. While it's a great service, it's pretty pricey: the cost to view one record is €5 (about

$6.60 as of this writing). But that's okay, because if you view eight records, it's €40. (I'll bet you can't guess how much it costs to view 20 records…that's right — €100.)

This pricing structure (pay-per-view) is popular in Europe, but not so much here in the US, as some of the European genealogy website heavyweights are finding. Americans are generally more comfortable with a subscription service (see: Ancestry.com, Fold3.org, etc.). Let's hope this pricing structure doesn't catch on in the United States (at least not at that cost level!).

The information provided is an abstract of the information on the records, and you can't look at the actual image, which is too bad.

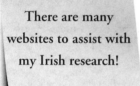

There are many websites to assist with my Irish research!

Going to Ireland

Okay, let's say you have this craving to go to Ireland, the land of your forefathers (as many individuals of Irish descent do). You want to do some real roll-up-your-sleeves research yourself. Can you do it? Of course. But first, do all you can to narrow your search before you go to Ireland. And how do you narrow your search? First of all, you need as much of the following information as you can get:

•Surname(s) of the individual(s) you are researching
•Names of parents, siblings, spouses (including maiden names of women), etc.
•County where they came from
•City or town they lived in
•Name of the parish they lived in
•Approximate years of critical events: birth, death, marriage, etc.

Even though you are armed with that information, don't go jump on an Aer Lingus flight and head for Ireland. Know what your options are before you go. Some options are:

1. **National Library of Ireland**, Kildare Street, Dublin 2, Ireland, *www.nli.ie/ en/family-history-introduction.aspx.* The e-mail address for their family history section is *genealogy@nli.ie/.* This is the national depository of many of Ireland's records on microfilm. It specializes in Catholic parish registers. The office is open to the public, and you can go here and pore over microfilmed records to your heart's content. Before you go, write to them to determine what records they have available for the parish or diocese where your family lived – include all the information you are looking for. Most of the parish records from around the country are contained here on microfilm.

The library also has land valuation records and tithe applotment records available for review. These records were compiled between 1823 and 1838 as a survey of titheable land in each parish. (They do not cover cities or towns). In general, the information contained in the Tithe Books is as follows: name of occupier, name of townland, acreage, classification of land, amount of tithe due.

The Land Valuation records are a record of the land and who lived on it between 1848 and 1864. Since many of Ireland's 19th-century genealogy records were destroyed, these records are a valuable substitute and provide at least some information to researchers.

2. If you know the parish where your family lived, it is possible that their names are recorded in the **local parish records**. Try and locate an address and send a letter to the local clergyman, specifying the information you are seeking, and asking whether they have records that the public can peruse. Most do, some do not. Don't just show up at the priest's door with a grin on your face and a story of your search for your great aunt Bridget Murphy (note: there are many Bridgets and many Murphys in Ireland…).

3. Ireland's **National Archives** houses many microfilmed records from throughout Ireland, including Church of Ireland parish registries, gravestone inscriptions, census returns, probate records, deeds and a host of other records. The address is National Archives, Bishop Street, Dublin 8, Ireland. Their genealogy section of their website is located at *www.nationalarchives.ie/ genealogy1/introduction-to-genealogy,* and their e-mail address is *mail@nationalarchives.ie.*

The records available at the National Archives includes tithing applotment records, land valuation records, the 1901 and 1911 Irish censuses, Ireland-Australia transportation records (1791 to 1853), estate, parish and marriage records.

4. The **Public Record Office of Northern Ireland (PRONI)** has microfilms of church records of all denominations for all of Northern Ireland as well as several of the counties of the Republic. The website for their genealogy section is *www.proni.gov.uk/index/family_history.htm.* They also have many of the same secular records as the National Archives, including gravestone inscriptions, census records, old age pension claims, tithe applotment books, etc.

Several of the more interesting collections they have at PRONI are the *Ulster Covenant, Freeholders' Records,* and *Will Calendars.* The former is a list of men and women – about a quarter of a million people – who signed the Ulster Covenant in 1912, a document that was a visible protest of Northern Irish residents who did not want to become part of the Irish Republic.

Freeholders' Records are records of men who held enough land (or had enough money) to be allowed to vote. The records run from 1727 through 1840. In addition to providing information about the voter and his land holdings, some of the records also include the names of those who were living in the home with him. When you search their database of freeholder records, you'll first receive a brief summary of the document. But clicking on *View Image* allows you to view the image itself, and that's usually where information about the freeholder's family is located.

Will calendars is a misleading name – it provides an abstract and actual images of wills of Northern Ireland residents between 1858 and 1900 – nearly 100,000 wills.

One of the best things about these three sets of records is that they are digitized and available online – some of the first on the Emerald Isle. Let's hope this trend catches on in Ireland!

Names

Below are first names you are likely to run into as you are researching your Irish ancestors. You may wonder why I am taking the time to provide Irish names for boys and girls for you. They speak English in Ireland, right? Yes and no. Yes – most of the Irish speak English. However, there are areas of Ireland designated as *Gaeltacht* – areas where the inhabitants usually speak Gaelic – also known as the Irish language. Through the centuries since the English occupied Ireland, many of the names adopted by the Irish have English origins. Many, however, have Gaelic origins. I told my wife that had I been as in touch with my Irish roots when we first married as I now am, at least several of our children would have carried Irish names: Maeve, Aiofe, and Siobhan for the girls and Aidan, Ciaran and Eamon for the boys are among the possibilities. (It is apparently a good thing I was happy with good old American names…my wife wasn't too sold on any of those names. I was able to get Teague approved as one of our son's middle names, however!)

Haillí na héireann ainmneacha chéad *(Irish boys first names)*
Aedan
Breandan
Cabhan
Carrig
Cathal
Cian
Ciaran
Coilin
Colm
Conall
Conan
Cormack
Darcy
Deaglan
Diarmuid
Donal
Eamonn
Eoghan
Faolan

Fergus
Finbar
Hugh
Jarlath
Liam
Lorcan
Malachi
Niall
Oisin
Padraig
Riordan

Cailíní na héireann ainmneacha chéad *(Irish girls first names)*

Aine	Granuaile
Aiofe	Kaitlyn
Aislin	Maebh
Branna	Maire
Briana	Meara
Brigid	Niamh
Caitronia	Nollaig
Colleen (of course!)	Nuala
Deirdre	Regan
Emer	Roisin
Eithne / Enya	Ryanne
Fianna	Sinead
Fiona	Siobhan
Fionnoula	Sheenagh
Gael	Teagan

10. YOUR ITALIAN ROOTS

In the 2010 US census of the United States, more than 18 million Americans indicated they were of Italian descent. That's a lot of people – about one in 20 – living in America that trace their roots back to that boot-shaped country in southwestern Europe.

Key Records
There are a number of key records available as you begin your search for your Italian roots. Following are some of those sources:

Censuses
The Italian government initiated formal censuses in 1871, and have continued them every ten years since then. The first four *censimenti* (censuses) were like the first six US censuses – they list only the head of household's name and then provide a tally of the number of other people in the household. The first Italian census to provide names, ages, birthplaces, and relationship to the head of the household is the 1911 Italian census.

Censuses for each area are generally kept at the local registrar's office as well as in the state archive of each province. Many of these records have been microfilmed and placed online for your viewing pleasure. For those that have not, you'll need to contact the local registrar or possibly the state archives for information about their collections.

Church Records
Well, you knew a predominantly Catholic country like Italy would have a great supply of church records that will assist genealogists, didn't you? And such is the case. The Catholic Church, that great genealogical record keeper through the ages, has not let us down in Italy. They did a fine job of

preserving genealogical information through their record keeping. These records extend back hundreds of years. In general, most Catholic churches began keeping records in the mid- to late 1500s, although a few began much earlier – in the 14th century. Many of these records are now online at services like FamilySearch.org and Ancestry.com.

Sometimes, church records were destroyed. Italy was the crossroads of a number of warring armies throughout history, and sometimes, churches (and their records) were casualties of the fighting. It is important to remember that often, duplicates of records were made and forwarded to the diocese to which parishes belonged. So if the parish where your ancestor was born, lived, married, and / or died had records that were destroyed, check with the local diocese for those records.

Many of the church records have indexes, and other do not. One researcher whose work I consulted on Italian church records said that often, a record may have no index, or it might even have multiple indexes. Most often, indexes use first names, not surnames. And — names are of course written in Italian, with some also written in Latin.

Many of these records have been microfilmed and / or put online. For those areas where they have not been made available, you will need to contact the local parish where your ancestor lived and where his / her records may be residing.

Civil Registration

The Italians, or more specifically genealogists doing genealogical research, have Napoleon Bonaparte to thank for the beginning of civil registration in Italy. When Napoleon defeated portions of Italy, he decreed that civil registration was to take place. This began in parts of Italy as early as 1804. When Napoleon was ousted in 1815, most areas of Italy ceased keeping civil records. But they were started once again in 1860 and continue to this day. Statute required each municipality (*comune*) to keep original records and forward copies to the courthouse. These civil registrations included information about births, deaths, marriages and marriage banns.

Generally speaking, most civil registration records are not available for viewing until 75 years after the event you're seeking (birth, death, marriage).

Marriage bann = public announcement of an upcoming marriage.

These are great records to find and peruse. I have had the opportunity to do so, and I would suggest you spend time reviewing any of a number of fine articles written on interpreting and understanding Italian handwriting! You can find a number of these articles on *FamilySearch.org* under their *Wiki* tab.

Many of the civil registrations taken at the local level have been microfilmed by various entities, including FamilySearch.org, and are available online. It's a lot easier and less expensive to find these records online or on microfilm; if you are unable to do so, then you'll need to contact the local registrar's office in the town where your ancestors lived.

Military Records
Often overlooked sources of genealogical information – for the men, anyway – are Italy's military records. National military registration began for all young men aged 18 in Italy in 1865. Their conscription records are complete with their name, birth date, address, parents, next of kin and other information pertinent to the military. These military records are held in each of the province archives locations across the country.

Province Archives
There are over 100 (110, to be exact) provinces within Italy, and each has an archives location. The provinces are part of twenty Italian regions. If you are unable to locate civil and church records in the town where your ancestors lived, you might reach out to the province archives offices for each province. The twenty regions in Italy are:

Abruzzo
Basilicata
Calabria
Campania

Emilia-Romagna
Friuli-Venezia Giulia
Lazio
Liguria
Lombardia
Marche
Molise
Piemonte
Puglia
Sardegna
Sicilia
Toscana
Trentino-Sud Tirol
Umbria
Valle d'Aosta / Valle d'Aoste
Veneto

Each province has their own website. A good website that provides links to all these provinces is *www.italywgw.org/province*. Following the links takes you to indexes for each province's genealogical collections, and then on to some of those collections – usually abstracts or transcriptions. Another good website for locating the state archives for each province is *www.italyworldclub.com/genealogy/archives*. They provide links to each of the regions, and each of those links in turn provides links to the archives in each province.

Sometimes multiple cities within each province have archives. One of the two websites listed in the paragraph above should help you learn where the province archives offices are for the areas of your ancestors' nativity.

The province archives are a great source for many Italian records – birth, marriage, death, military, censuses, etc. Be sure and check them out.

Helpful Websites for Italian Research
Following are websites that will be helpful as you venture into Italy in search of your ancestors:

Ancestry.com
As of this writing, Ancestry.com's international subscription edition includes an extensive collection of Italian records, including:

• Potenza, Basilicata civil registration, 1961 to 1938
• Como and Lecco, Lombardy civil registration records, 1866 to 1936
• Falerna, Catanzaro, Calabria civil registration records, 1810 to 1936
• Palermo, Sicily birth records index, 1876 to 1885
• Pavia, Lombardy civil registration records, 1866 to 1937

Italian Genealogy — *www.italiangenealogy.com* – this is a great website, representing one of the things I like best about doing genealogy – genealogists helping one another. This website brings together over 34,000 genealogists and family researchers, and provides opportunities for them to ask and answer questions about Italian research. Following are the categories in which people request and receive information:

• Italian Genealogy (searching for a surname? Need more info on family heritage?)
• Locations in Italy (Need more information on a town or village in Italy? Need help locating a town?)
• Italian History and Culture
• Emigration, Immigration, Naturalization and Italian citizenship
• Italian language, handwriting , script & translations

As I perused this website, I couldn't help but notice the amount of traffic and frequency of use: most categories had active conversations (questions and answers) going on, often within mere minutes of when I first started checking things out. I think it will be a great website to have in your back pocket (or *favorites* list) as you venture into the world of Italian genealogical research.

Italian Genealogical Group — *www.italiangen.org* is a great website for Italian genealogical research. It is based out of New York City, and it has a tremendous number of links related to Italian research. Most are US records – immigration and naturalization records, databases with Italian-surnamed individuals, etc. One page (*www.italiangen.org/Towns.stm*) is particularly useful for those reaching back to Italy for research. It is a data base of over 8,000 comunes (communes) / towns in Italy and their correct spellings, along with their province.

Italy Gen Web — *www.italywgw.org* is another one of those great websites available for those researching their Italian roots. It includes a quick overview to the types of Italian records you can expect and links to various Italian records (birth, marriage, death, immigration, ship manifests, etc.). It is not an extensive website, but it is nicely done and navigation is easily intuitive.

Italy World Genealogy — *www.italyworldclub.com/genealogy*. I like this site. The site listed is a page off the larger Italy World website, but I think it provides a good entrance into the world of Italian genealogy. One of the nice items on this website is a list of surnames that are common to various comunes (towns), provinces and regions.

FamilySearch.org – *www.familysearch.org* has a number of documents and video courses about Italian research, and all are available to the public for free. There is a one-hour video on beginning Italian research that is quite excellent. It is located at *https://www.familysearch.org/learningcenter/lesson/basic-italian-research/246*. There are also a number of videos centered on learning to work with Italian script on the same website. At the time of this writing, they were two of the half dozen or so video courses on doing Italian research. These courses can be found by clicking the *Search* tab on the *FamilySearch.org* home page, and then clicking on *Wiki* on the next page and entering *Italian research.*

From the same *Wiki* tab, you can find nearly 800 articles on doing Italian research, including such titles as *Italian Censuses, Italian Handwriting, Italy Church Records, Italy Websites*, etc. To locate these short lessons, go to *www.familysearch.org*, and click on the *Search* tab, then click on *Wiki*. In the search box, enter *Italy*, or something more specific: *Italy Church Records*, for example.

Also, at the time of this writing, there well over 3 million names in FamilySearch's various Italian collections including the following:

- Italy births and baptisms, 1806 to 1900
- Italy deaths and burials, 1809 to 1900
- Italy Catania, Arcidiocesi di Catani Civil Registration, 1820 to 1905
- Italy Catania, Arcidiocesi di Catania, Aatholic Church records 1515 to 1941
- Italy, Cuneo, Civil Registration, 1795 to 1915

If you have been unsuccessful in finding information about your Italian ancestors on the various websites listed above, it may be time to reach out to some of the places those records are held. Following are sample letters you might use to request information from the Italian authorities. Letters written in English are often discarded and not replied to; therefore you would do better attempting to request those records in Italian! Also, I suggest keeping the letters simple and to the point!

June 15, 2013

Good day,
I live in the United States. My ancestors are from Italy. I would like to learn about them.

Here is the information I have about my ancestors that were born in Italy:

Last name:

First Name:

Date of birth (approximate):
Place of birth:

Father's given name and surname:

Mother's given name and surname: unknown

I request complete transcriptions of the original records.

Please tell me the cost of these services. The most I want to pay is US$_____. If you send me a bill for the genealogy research, I will pay it. I understand you will not send the information until after I pay.

My address is:
(Put your mailing address here)
Thank you,
Daniel Quillen
wdanielquillen@gmail.com

And here it is in Italian:

15 Giugno 2013

Buongiorno,

Io vivo negli Stati Uniti. I miei antenati erano dalla Italia. Vorrei imparare su di loro.

I includere le informazioni che ho sui miei antenati che sono nati in Italia:

Cognome:
Nome:

Data di nascita (approssimativa):

Luogo di nascita:

Padre nome e cognome:

Della madre nome e cognome: sconosciuto

Chiedo le trascrizioni complete di documenti originali.

Per favore fatemi sapere il costo di questi servizi. Il più pagare è di $ _____. Se mi mandi un conto per raccogliere ricerca genealogica, la cambiale. Capisco che tu non inviare informazioni fino a dopo che ho pagato.

Il mio indirizzo è:
(Put your mailing address here)

Grazie,

Daniel Quillen
wdanielquillen@gmail.com

Parole, parole, parole *(Words, words, words)*
Below are words you are likely to run into as you research Italian records.

anno – year
atto di nascita – birth records
bambino – baby (you knew that, didn't you?!)
battesimo – baptism
certificato di morte – death certificate
circondario – district
città — city
civile – civil
cognome – surname
età — age
famiglia – family
figli – children
figlia – daughter
figlio – son
fu – deceased, late
genitori — parents
giorno – day
madre – mother
maritata – married to
marito – husband
matrimonio – marriage, matrimony

mese — month
morte – death
morto – died
nascità – birth
nata / nato – born (female / male)
nom / nome – name
parrochia – parish
sesso – sex, gender
sposato – married
stato — status
stato civile – civil status
vedova – widow
vedovo – widower

Mesi dell'anno *(Months of the year)*
Gennaio — January
Febbraio — February
Marzo — March
Aprile — April
Maggio — May
Giugno — June
Luglio — July
Agosto – August
Settembre — September
Ottobre — October
Novembre — November
Dicembre — December

Names
Below are first names you are likely to run into as you are researching your Italian ancestors. I have found that at least being familiar with the spelling of common names has helped me decipher many genealogy records through the years.

Ragazzi italiani primi nomi *(Italian boys' first names)*
Adriano
Alanzo

Alessandro
Amadeo
Andrea
Arrigo
Arturo
Bartolomeo
Benedetto
Benito
Bernardo
Carlo
Constantin
Cristoforo
Edoardo
Enrico
Ernesto
Federico
Fiorello
Giacobbe
Giacomo
Gino
Giorgio
Giovanni
Guglielmo
Guiseppe
Lanzo
Luigi
Marco
Matteo
Paolo
Patrizio
Pietro
Rafaelo
Riccardo
Vittorio

Primi nomi di ragazze Italiane *(Italian girls' first names)*
Abriana

Agnesia
Aida
Andriana
Annamaria
Antea
Anzola
Aryanna
Belaflore
Cadiana
Ciana
Donata
Donia
Fabrizia
Fiorilla
Galiana
Galicia
Gaspara
Graziella
Guilietta
Isabella
Iseppa
Jianna
Justyna
Leandra
Livia
Loredana
Matalia
Rosina
Savia
Sophia
Violetta
Zanobia

11. YOUR POLISH ROOTS

In the 2010 US census of the United States, ten million Americans indicated they were of Polish descent. It is interesting to look at a map of the United States that has been super-imposed with the percentage of each state's population that claims Polish ancestry. New York and Illinois each has nearly one million individuals of Polish ancestry living within their state boundaries, followed by Michigan and Pennsylvania, with between 800,000 and 900,000 Polish descendants living within their borders. New Jersey, Wisconsin, and California each has in the neighborhood of 500,000 Polish descendants, with Ohio and Florida coming in with populations in excess of 400,000 Polish descendants. Most of the other northeastern states (Connecticut, Maryland, Massachusetts, New Hampshire and New Jersey) all have healthy numbers of Polish descendants living within their states as well.

With so many descendants of Polish ancestors living in the United States, it just seems to make sense to begin here and see what information you can glean from existing US records, rather than immediately jumping overseas to find ancestral records. I know it's not quite as spectacular as planning a trip to Poland, but it's a lot less expensive and may help you find the correct doors to open in Poland before you go.

Wow – lots of Polish Americans in the midwest and north-east!

As with all the nationalities discussed in this book, before you pack your suitcase and head out to Poland, you should do absolutely as much research as you can from the comfort of your own home. If you are focusing on this chapter, it's a decent bet that at least some of your Polish ancestors entered, and / or lived in one of those states mentioned in the opening paragraph of this chapter.

And that's where your research should begin. Immigration and naturalization records, censuses, obituaries, county histories, etc., that can be found right here in the United States may yield genealogical nuggets that will allow you to begin putting together the puzzle pieces of these Polish ancestors of yours. Let's discuss a few of those sources.

Your Own Records
Don't be in such a rush that you overlook records you may have at your very fingertips – or the fingertips of one or more of your close relatives. *Someone* in the family may have copies of birth and death certificates, marriage certificates and obituaries. Don't overlook these important documents, as they may shed a great deal of light on your ancestors and their origins.

Often, these records will be written in Polish, or German, or perhaps even Russian, depending on the portion of Poland your relatives came from, and when. Your first charge is to find out if any of your relatives have these documents. Begin with the oldest ones first, and work your way down through aunts, uncles, cousins, etc.

If you find documents you cannot understand due to language barriers, there are a plethora of resources to turn to for assistance. *Www.freetranslation.com* or *www.translate.google.com* are good places to start. Polish genealogical societies may have members who will be happy to assist in the translation of such documents, often for free, or for a modest donation.

Censuses
Remember – a series of censuses in the early 20th century asked questions of all US inhabitants that identified not only country of birth for individuals, but also for their parents. The 1920 and 1930 censuses also asked what year individuals immigrated and the year of their naturalization, if they were naturalized.

If you have read any of my other books, you know I love to use my ancestors to demonstrate various research techniques. Unfortunately, my relatives all come from a little to the west of Poland: Ireland (mostly), a few from Britain and one black sheep that came from France. But I want to provide some tangible examples, so I searched my brain and remembered a dear friend from many years and miles ago. His name is Gary Czarnecki, and he is of Polish descent. So I will see if I can't use some of his relatives to demonstrate a few Polish research tactics.

I hop on Ancestry.com and launch a query for Anthony Czarnecki. I am immediately successful with the following information:

In the 1930 US Census, Cook County, Illinois (Poles in Chicago?! Go figure...), I find the following family:

Czarnecki, Anthony	Head	52
Sabrina	Wife	48
James E.	Son	19
Anthony P	Son	15
Joseph N.	Son	12
Valentine	Father	81
Hahn, Helen E.	Mother-in-law	67

I further discover that Anthony and Valentine, his father, both immigrated to the United States in 1885, and both have been naturalized. This is key information for us. A date of 1885 gives us a lower end of the timeframe we'll want to check for immigration and naturalization papers as well as passenger lists. Based on their ages at the time of immigration, Anthony must have been around five years old, and Valentine must have been about 36 years of age. They both came from and were born in Poland. Helen Hahn, Anthony's mother-in-law, was born in Illinois, but both her parents were born in Poland. Anthony's wife Sabrina was born in Nebraska, but her father was born in Poland and her mother was born in Illinois. Both Anthony's father and mother-in-law have lost their spouses – they are listed as a widower and widow in the census. We also learn that Anthony was married at age 32 and his wife at age 28. I also discover that Anthony was a veteran, and he fought in World War I. I tuck this information away, and will later check to see if I can find his draft registration card. The family is beginning to take shape.

Okay – that's very interesting, but Poland is a big place, and I would like to see if I can find a little more specific place for these folks.

Let's check out the 1920 Census for Cook county and see if we can find this family again. Sure enough, in the Cook county, Illinois Census for 1920, we find:

Czarnecki, Anthony	Head	42
Sabrina	Wife	38
James	Son	9
Anthony	Son	5
Joseph	Son	2

This family – younger by ten years, of course, seems to be doing well. I do not see Valentine or Helen – Anthony's father and mother-in-law. They are probably living with their spouses, and unless I miss my guess, they are nearby. I take a moment and scan the census pages around the Anthony Czarnecki family, but this time no luck.

Passports

As I am perusing the ancestry website, I note that Anthony completed a passport application between 1914 and 1925. Passports can often provide great globs of information, so I head there to see what I can find about Mr. Czarnecki.

On March 14, 1922, naturalized citizen Anthony Czarnecki applied for a passport with the Cook County Courthouse. Here's what he wrote:

> I solemnly swear that I was born at <u>Posen, Poland</u>, on or about the <u>18th</u> day of January, 1<u>878</u>; that my father, <u>Walenty Czarnecki</u> was born in <u>Poland, then under German rule</u>! That he immigrated to the United States, sailing on board the <u>German Liner</u> from <u>Bremen</u> on or about May 1884….

It went on to say that both he and his father had lived continuously in the United States since their arrival, and that they had both been naturalized before the Cook County Circuit Court on the 28th day of October, 1890.

The back page of the passport application provides me a little insight into this ancestor. At the time of application (1922), he is 44 years old, is 5'6 1/2" tall and has a fair complexion. There is even a photograph of him!

You may have noted that in the 1930 Census, Anthony's father's name was Valentine, but in Anthony's passport application, his father is named Walenty. That is because Walenty is Polish, and Valentine is English for Walenty. Mystery solved.

Obituaries / Death Notices

Obituaries can provide tremendous amounts of genealogical information, information that may have been lost from other records. I have seen obituaries that provided extensive detail on locations of birth and marriage, as well as the locations of the births of every child born to a couple. They will often include information about the deceased's parents and even siblings, along with information about where to find information on them through tidbits of information about where they grew up, when they came from Poland to the United States, etc. Following is an example of an obituary.

To all relatives and acquaintances we report the sad news that our most beloved mother, sister and grandmother:

The late Iwona (Klepacki) Wozniak
Passed away after a short illness on January 23, 1940, aged 82 years.

The funeral will be held on Friday, January 26 at 10:30am at St. Stanislaw Kostka. Interment will take place at St. Wojeiech's cemetery (also known as St. Adelbert's cemetery).

We invite you to join the family to celebrate the life and mourn the passing of our wonderful mother and grand-mother:

Children and spouses: Feliks (Elzbieta), Grzegorz (Zuzanna), Izabella (Piotr Simkovski), Jozef (Rozalia), Alicja (Michal Wocjik).

Sisters and brothers-in-law: Anna (Andrzej) Kowalski, Ewa (Lukasz) Szymanski, Beatrycze (Jerzy)Wozniak

Brothers and sisters-in-law: Hajnrich (Hanna), Iwan (Kaja)

And thirty-seven grandchildren and 14 great grandchildren

Iwona was preceded in death by the love of her life, Feliks. They made a home and a life together that blessed all our lives. She and Feliks were both born in Gdansk and immigrated to America in 1897 with their six small children.

She will be missed.

Obituaries can be found a myriad of places: Polish newspaper archives, city newspaper archives, town or county biographies, etc. Check with local Polish genealogical societies for obituary archives they may have created in the area where your ancestors lived.

When you are looking for obituaries and death records for your deceased ancestors, be open to English translations of Polish names. As in the case of Walenty / Valentine Czarnecki, I found various records for him under one or the other name: Valentine Czarnecki, Walenty Czarnecki. There are any number of Internet sites that can assist with translation of Polish names. Some are obvious: Dawid / David, Feliks / Felix, Frydrych – Frederick, Szymon / Simon, Pawel / Paul, Piotr / Peter. Others are not so obvious:

Boleslaw / William, Jerzy / George, Wojciech / Albert, etc. A good site I found to assist with this is *polandpoland.com/common_polish_names.html*

Passenger Lists

We note from the 1920 and 1930 censuses that Walenty and Anthony Czarnecki immigrated to America in 1885 aboard a German liner that departed from Bremen. So we want to check a couple passenger lists. The most likely landing spot would have been New York, and since Ellis Island wasn't yet opened, we'll check its predecessor, Castle Garden. Boston, Baltimore and Philadelphia are also possible ports, and we will check them if Castle Garden doesn't yield any information.

As I dig a bit, I find Anthony landing in New York in 1916, when he was 38 years old. So this is a subsequent trip after his initial trip. However, he also states on the ship's manifest that he was naturalized under his father's naturalization, which occurred October 28, 1890 at the Circuit Court of Cook County, Chicago.

World War I & World War II Draft Registration

I remembered that Anthony indicated on one of the censuses that he was a veteran of the World War. I was able to locate his draft registration cards in Ancestry.com. It merely confirmed the information I already know – his name, birth date, address in Chicago and his wife's name. It also confirms for me that he gained his US citizenship by virtue of his father's naturalization.

He also was required to register for the old man's draft around World War II time, and again, no new information was found, but I was able to confirm the earlier information he provided.

War and Partitioning of Poland

Poland seems to be a crossroads in Europe...but unfortunately a crossroads of invading armies, or armies that were headed elsewhere to invade other countries. Unfortunately, Poland just seemed to be in the way.

Without spending a lot of time on history here in this chapter, Poland suffered through three or four (depending on who was counting) partitions.

The first was in 1772, when Poland was partitioned among the Russians, Prussia and Austria. Nearly two decades later in 1790, Russia and Prussia again partitioned Poland. A scant five years later, the three original partitioners eradicated the commonwealth of Poland by dividing her land among themselves. In the end, Russia claimed nearly two thirds of the former Polish Commonwealth, Prussia took about 20% and Austria ended up with about 15%.

After the partitions, the following provinces were claimed by the following countries:

Russia	Prussia	Austria
Bessarabia	Brandenburg	Bohemia
Grodno	East Prussia	Bukovina
Kalisz	Posen / Poznan	Galicia
Kielce	Mecklenberg	Hungary
Kovno	Saxony	Moravia
Kurland	Silesia	
Lomza	West Prussia (formerly Gdansk)	
Lubin		
Minsk		
Piotrkow		
Podole		
Plock		
Siedice		
Suwalki		
Vilebsk		
Vilnius		
Volynia		
Warszawa		

At the time of the Napoleonic Wars, boundaries were again shifted, and Russia ended up with about 82% of the land of former Poland, Austria controlled 11% and Prussia 7%.

So why do I bother you with this information? Because once you leave the borders in search of your ancestors in Poland, you will need to have some idea what partitioned portion of Poland your ancestors hailed from. This will help you prepare for the types of records that will be available, and the language you'll need to understand those records.

> Sometimes birth places will be recorded as Poland, Germany, Poland, Russia or Poland, Austria.

Genealogical records can be found for your Polish ancestors in Poland, but also in Germany and areas that used to be called Prussia.

Polish Records

As you search through the records available right here in the good old USA, you have hopefully gleaned a bucket load of information that you can now use to begin searching for your ancestors in Polish documents. These documents may be currently existing in Poland, may have been microfilmed by the LDS Church or put online by any number of subscription services. So how do you get access to those documents? You're probably not fluent in Polish, so how would you go about requesting information from Polish government authorities? All valid questions – let's see if I can answer some of them.

Notwithstanding the war difficulties that came Poland's way through the years, their records are amazingly intact and available. There are a great number of websites that provide information about Polish records, where they are and how to obtain copies of them. Following are some of the better ones:

Federation of Eastern European Family History Societies (FEEFHS): *http://feefhs.org* is a great site, and appears several times in this book. It is a great place to start in trying to noodle through all the places you may be able to find Polish records. A link within the home page allows you to discover a large variety of Polish records.

FamilySearch – *www.familysearch.org* provides great assistance in researching Polish records. From a thirty-year microfilming project in Poland, they have an extensive array of records just waiting to be tapped. The records are of course in Polish, so be sure and check out the key words guide of Polish genealogical words at the end of this chapter. The vast majority of the Polish records available through the LDS Church are on microfilm, and can either be viewed at the Family History Library in Salt Lake City, or can be ordered for a small fee (covering postage) for viewing at any of over 4,500 Family History Centers (FHC) located throughout the world (but most of them are in the United States). If you order a microfilm, it will arrive in about a week and will be available for your perusal for six weeks.

Of particular interest is a link from FEEFHS to an LDS publication that assists you in writing letters requesting records: *http://feefhs.org/guides/Polish.pdf*. It contains standard phrases that can be used for requesting vital records documents from Polish authorities.

FamilySearch.org – **FamilySearch** has a number of documents and video courses about Polish research, and all are available to the public for free. I found the following video course especially helpful in understanding Polish research: *https://www.familysearch.org/learningcenter/lesson/polish-ancestry/87*. At the time of this writing, it was one of 145 video courses on doing Polish research (some were more focused on Polish research only, while others contained references to Polish research in videos about research in other countries). These courses can be found from the *Search* tab on the FamilySearch.org home page, and then by clicking *Wiki*.

On the *Wiki* tab, type *Polish research* into the Search box. If you do that, you'll be treated to (as of this writing) over 200 articles on Polish research.

PolandGenWeb — *www.rootsweb.ancestry.com/~polwgw/Research.html*. This is another great website for learning about the locations of Polish records.

JewishGen—Polish Vital records page: *www.jewishgen.org/infofiles/polandv.html*. This well-written website (thanks Warren Blatt!) provides great information about where to find Jewish records in Poland.

Places to Search

Following are a number of places to launch your requests for birth and death certificates, marriage certificates, etc.

Polish State Archives

Polish vital records older than 100 years old are kept in the Polish State Archives in Warsaw (*Warszawa*). The website for the state archives is *http://archiwa.gov.pl/pl/*. If you aren't fluent in Polish, click the small English-flag icon at the top left of the page, and you'll be treated to an English translation of the site (good deal!).

Information about the process for getting vital records information can be obtained by writing or e-mailing:

Archival Information Centre
2D Rakowiecka Street,
02-517 Warszawa, Poland
e-mail: *ndap@archiwa.gov.pl*

There is a lengthy list of archival locations that is provided on the website – be sure and check the list out, as it may get you closer to the exact place where the records you seek are residing. A number of years ago, the Polish Archives began a program that requires all requests for vital records to be directed to the archival location where the information resides. There is a list on the Polish State Archives webpage that provides the links to the various archival locations: *archiwa.gov.pl/index.php?option=com_contentc&view=article&id=381&Itemid=183.*)

As of this writing, the cost to research documents is $15 an hour, with a minimum deposit of $30 to get started. It may be prudent to provide a "not-to-exceed" limit on your records request.

Church Records

As about any place else in the world, Polish church records often antedate civil records (and in many instances, they *were* the civil records!). Following is information about how and where to find some of these records:

Catholic Church — The Roman Catholic Church (*Rzymsko-Katolicki*) has had a significant presence in Poland through the centuries. Their records in many instances date back to the mid-to-late 1500s. Church records may be kept at the parish or diocese level, and / or they may be found at the state archival location. Beginning in the late 1700s, churches were conscripted (so to speak) as the record keepers for the government, and their records often formed the basis for forced conscription of Polish citizens into military service. Those records were often copied at the local levels and provided on up the line to the diocese as well as the civil authorities.

In the earlier years (prior to 1772 – the date of the first partition of Poland), the records were generally kept in Latin. After the partition, the records were kept in the language of the ruling government: Russian, German, Polish and some even in French.

The following website provides a list of addresses and contact information for all the Catholic dioceses (dioci?) in Poland: *www.opoka.org.pl/struktury_kosciola/diecezje/index.html*. Most of the entries provide mailing addresses as well as e-mail addresses.

Greek Catholic Church – Grecko—Katolicka – also kept records. Their records were generally written in Slavic, Polish, Ukrainian and Latin. A great website to learn more about records kept by the Greek Catholic church can be found at *www.lemko.org/genealogy/galiciapl.html*.

Evangelical (Luthern) Church — ewangelicko-augsburski – the records kept by the Lutheran Church in Poland mirror the records kept by other churches. The records are generally kept at the local parish level. A good site for more information on where these parishes are, and how to contact them is *www.luteranie.pl/pl/index.php?D=113*. Lutheran records were generally kept in the language of the local populace.

Jewish — zydowskiona — records were also voluminous. One of the best websites I ran across for Jewish records is listed earlier in this chapter – JewishGen. So you don't have to flip back to the page, here is the website: *www.jewishgen.org/infofiles/polandv.html*.

Many of these church records were microfilmed by the LDS Church, and those records are available for the general public to review either in the LDS Church Family History Library in Salt Lake City, Utah, or they can be requested to be sent to any of over 4,500 Family History Centers – local branches of the FHL.

Civil Records

As mentioned earlier, many Church records became civil records, but there were other civil records that were kept also. Polish civil records generally fall into one of three categories, all evolving around the partition of Poland.

Congress Poland (Russian control) — In the early 1800s, Napoleon Bonaparte introduced civil registration into Poland. When the Russians began occupying Poland, they liked the Napoleonic system and left it in place. It's actually a pretty unique format for civil records – the information is in standard paragraph format that included an introduction, information about the person and the event (birth, marriage, death) with the information in a standard place on the form. There was also a section that included the names of the witnesses. Prior to 1868, these records were kept in Polish, and between 1868 and 1918, it was kept in Russian (think: Cyrillic alphabet!).

Galicia (Prussian / German control) – these records can generally be found in either Latin or German. Beginning in the 1790s, these records were used for military conscription purposes.

Prussia (German control) – as you'd expect, most of these records were kept in German. Civil records in this area began in 1874.

Emigration Records – Poles emigrated most often through Amsterdam, Antwerp, Bremen and Hamburg. A few also left from Rotterdam. Unfortunately, few of the records from Amsterdam and Antwerp have survived, and all the Bremen records were destroyed. That leaves the Hamburg passenger lists as one of the few major records groups available, but there are considerable numbers of immigrants listed in those lists. Please see the coverage of the *Hamburg Passenger Lists* in Chapter 8.

In-Country Research Services

There are a number of companies within Poland that will provide genealogical research for you. If you've hit a brick wall and can go no further, you may wish to use their services. The *Piast Nobility Genealogical Center* in Warsaw is one of those companies. They can be reached at:

Osrodek Badan Genealogicznych "Piast"
skr. poczt. 9
ul. Podchorazych 89 m. 9
00-957 Warszawa 36
Polska

Their website is *www.piast.waw.pl/*, and their e-mail address is *obgpiast@wp.pl*. They will do the leg-work for you – traveling to the various archival locations in search of the vital records of your noble ancestors. Their reports are available in Polish, or for a translation fee, in English.

Their rates are not cheap, but they may provide an option for you. They require a $20 retainer, then charge their services at $12 an hour for research and compilation, $8 an hour for traveling to the location of some archives, along with 30 cents per kilometer. If they find and abstract information from birth, death or marriage certificates, the cost is $10 per abstract.

> I might want to consider a professional Polish genealogist to assist if I run into brick walls.

Marriage databases – there are a number of projects underway to capture and make available online marriage information for several areas of Poland. Below are a few, but there are others that are available. Just Google *Marriage database Poland* and see what sites come up.

Poznan Marriage Database – this is a great website, listing in excess of 750,000 marriages that occurred during the 19th century in Posen (now Poznan), Poland.

Geneteka baza Poliskiego Towarzystwa Genealogicznego is one of the more prolific websites for locating Polish marriage records. It is located at *http://www.geneteka.genealodzy.pl/index.php?op=se,* and offers nearly 7 million marriage records. That's a lot of Polish marriages! (Note – this is a great website, but sometimes the *Translate* application doesn't work very well. Until you begin recognizing common words, you may need to cut and paste some of the words from the form into *www.freetranslation.com* to discover what information the site is requesting.)

Military records – these records are available for all the partitioned areas of Poland. As with church records, many of these military records have been microfilmed by the LDS Church.

If you have been unsuccessful in finding the ancestral information you have been seeking, it may be time to search for those records in Poland. Following are sample letters you might use to request information from the Polish authorities. Letters written in English are often discarded and not replied to; therefore you would do better attempting to request those records in Polish!

June 15, 2013

Dear Sir,
I live in the United States, but my ancestry is from Poland, and I would like to know more about my Polish ancestors.

The following persons are my ancestors who were born in Poland. I will give all the vital data about them that I have.

Walenty Czarnecki

Date of birth (approximate): July 1, 1949

Place of birth: Gdansk

Father's given name and surname: Jerzy Czarnecki

Mother's given name and surname: unknown

Please send me a complete extract of the birth or christening record of (1) this person. (2) these persons.

Please let me know the cost of your help and how I can pay.

My address is:

Thank you,

Daniel Quillen
wdanielquillen@gmail.com

And now in Polish:

15 Czerwiec 2013

Szanowny Panie,

Mieszkam w Stanach Zjednoczonych, ale moi przodkowie sąpolskiego pochodzenia. Chciałbym (chciałabym, if you are a female) dowiedziećsię więcej o moich polskich przodkach.

Następuja ce osoby sa moimi przodkami urodzonymi w Polsce. Podaję wszystkie dane jakie mam o nich.

Walenty Czarnecki

Data urodzenia (w przybliżeniu): 1 Lipiec 1849

Miejsce urodzenia: Gdańsk

Imii nazwisko ojca: Jerzy Czarnecki

Imiei nazwisko panieńskie matki: nieznany

Proszeo przesłanie mi pełnego odpisu świadectwa urodzenia albo chrztu (1) tej osoby. (2) tych osób.

Prosze napisać do mnie, ile sie należy za pomoc iw jaki sposób moge za nią zapłacić.

Mój adres:

Your name
Address
City, State, zip Code
USA

Dziękujemy za

Daniel Quillen
wdanielquillen@gmail.com

Thank you, LDS Church, for the translation assistance. I cobbled together the Polish letter above using the sample phrases they listed in their document, as well as using *Google Translate* and *www.freetranslation.com*. A couple of things about your letters: do your best to use the symbols in the Polish alphabet. This may require you to add dots, accents and curly-cues to words that are typed. Or you can cut and paste them from sites like *www.freetranslation.com* or *www.translate.google.com*. Use the Polish name of your ancestor if you can find it. There are several good websites that can assist you in finding the Polish equivalent to an English name. Just Google *Polish name translation.*

If possible, seek out e-mail addresses for the places you will be sending your request. However, many will not have e-mail, or may not publish their e-mail addresses. Include your e-mail address after your name, in case they do have e-mail and are willing to correspond with you in that manner.

Słowa, słowa, słowa *(Words, words, words)*
Below are words you are likely to run into as you research Polish records.

akt – record
babcia – grandmother
biskup – bishop
brat – brother
certyfikat – certificate, record
chlopiec – boy
chrzest – baptism
chrzestna -- godmother
chrestny – godfather
ciotka – aunt
córkadla – daughter
dorosłych – adult
data – date

dniu – date
dziadek – grandfather
dziewczyna -- daughter
dzielnica – district / ward
ewangelicko-augsburski – Lutheran
gmina – district / community
kapłan – priest
kobieta – woman
ksqidz – priest, father
łoa – illegitimate
loza -- illegitimate
małżeństwo -- marriage
malżonka -- wife
matka – mother
mqż – husband
miejscowości – village, town
miesiąc – month
nazwa – name
nazwisko -- surname
nieslubny – illegitimate
ojca – father
ojciec – father
panstwo – nation / state
płeć – sex, gender
pochowany -- buried
pogrzeb – burial
probosczc – pastor
rabin – rabbi
rodzice – parents
rodzina – family
rok – year
rzymsko-katolicki – Roman Catholic
siostra – sister
stryj – uncle (paternal)
syn – son
synowa – daughter-in-law

szwagier – brother-in-law
smierć – death
ślub – wedding
urodzenie – born (abbreviated ur.)
wdowa – widow
wdowiec – widower
wesele – wedding
wiek – age
wies – village
wnuk – grandson
wojewodztwo – province
wuj – uncle (maternal)
z – from, nee
zamezna – married woman
żeński(a) -- female
zgon -- death
zgonu – death certificate
zmarł – died
zmarły – deceased
żona -- wife
żonaty – married
żyd – Jew
żydowskiona -- Jewish

Names

Below are first names you are likely to run into as you are researching your Polish ancestors. I have found that at least being familiar with the spelling of common names has helped me decipher many genealogy records through the years

Polscy chłopcy nazwiska *(Polish boys first names)*
Aleksy
Amadej
Andrzej
Bazyli
Bolek

Boleslaw
Cezar
Czeslaw
Dariusz
Dawid
Donat
Dorofiej
Feliks
Fryderyk
Frydrych
Gabryjel
Grzegorz
Hajnrich
Iwan
Jacek
Jerzy
Jozef
Konstantyn
Krystyn
Lukasz
Marek
Michal
Pawel
Piotr
Szczepan
Szymon
Wawrzyniec
Wojciech

Polskie dziewczyny nazwiska *(Girls first names)*
Adelajda
Albino
Alicja
Anastazja
Augustyna
Beatrycze

Cecylia
Czeslawa
Dorota
Dyta
Elzbieta
Felicyta
Gabrysia
Grazyna
Hanna
Honorata
Iwona
Izabella
Izolda
Jadzia
Janina
Jowita
Justyna
Kaja
Kasia
Katarzyna
Konstancja
Krystiana
Leokadia
Luiza
Rozalia
Zofia
Zuzanna

12. YOUR PORTUGUESE ROOTS

Portugal poses a conundrum for those seeking ancestors within her boundaries. Most of the heavyweight genealogy sites with which I have always had success come up relatively empty when it comes to Portuguese research. Sites like FamilySearch.org and Ancestry.com, for example, have very little. As of this writing, Ancestry has no records online, and FamilySearch has very limited information, consisting mostly of lists of websites that might help. But I've scoured the Internet trying to find a few things that will be of value to you as you research your Portuguese ancestors. Many of the records, however, are not online.

Because of the scarcity of access to Portuguese records, I recommend making a concerted effort to find whatever you can from American records. While this is important for all European research, it is especially so for Portuguese research. Ships passenger lists, immigration and naturalization records, death and marriage certificates may help you unlock the secrets to your Portuguese ancestors' lives. A marriage certificate, for example, may identify the parish church where your ancestors were married. Armed with the name of that church and town, you can conduct a thorough search of the Internet targeted specifically to that particular place. If nothing results online, then a letter may be sent – with hopes, prayers and a little bit of money – to the church itself.

Before we get to some records, following is a little information that may assist you in your Portuguese ancestral search:

In Portuguese, it is common for individuals to have two given names and two family surnames. Generally speaking, when two surnames are listed, the first is the mother's family name and the second the father's surname. However, sometimes the names are reversed, so be cautious in making the hard-and-fast assumption that the first surname is the mother's maiden name. But use it as a clue as you do further research. Usually, when a woman married she took her husband's surname as her last name, although on occasion that was not the case.

Compared to American naming norms, the Portuguese are very flexible, which of course can drive genealogists to the brink of insanity. Several hundred years ago – right at the time when you may be doing your research – it was not uncommon for boys to take their father's surname as their own, but the daughters often took their mother's maiden name for their surname. It was fairly common to find families listed with the boys and girls having different surnames. This can of course be confusing! Just take good notes, and understand you may have to roll up your sleeves extra high to get to the bottom of some of these family relationships!

Portuguese law allows up to four family names to be used in naming an individual. Sometimes the first two names come from the mother and the last two from the father, although the reverse is true. However, it could just as easily be one name from one parent and three names from another parent. Given those potential scenarios, using Portuguese naming nomenclature, my names could be:

- William Daniel *Quillen* (father's surname)
- William Daniel *Lowrance* **Quillen** (*mother's surname*, **father's surname**)
- Daniel *Hudson Lowrance* **Cunningham Quillen** (*mother's two surnames*, **father's two surnames**)
- Daniel *Cunningham Quillen* **Hudson Lowrance** (*father's two surnames*, **mother's two surnames**)
- Daniel *Lowrance* **Cunningham McCollough Quillen** (*mother's surname*, **father's three surnames**)

And so forth! One of my mathematician readers can probably weigh in on the number of possible names that could be derived if you assume the use of one or two given names and four surnames, and the varying alternative uses of names available. The nice thing is – generally the surnames being used must be the names of progenitors. So if you find an ancestor with four surnames – rejoice – you're that much closer to identifying generations further up the family tree.

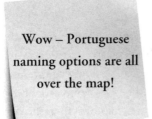

Wow – Portuguese naming options are all over the map!

Key Records

As discussed above, the genealogy world hasn't flocked to Portugal to microfilm or get their records online, but I was able to find a few that may be of interest:

Censuses

Portuguese census and notary records are available, although most are not online. They are kept at the National and District archives locations. Some of the notary records extend back to the 1300s.

Church Records

As with most European countries with heavy Catholic populations (Portugal is 94% Catholic), church records (birth, marriage, death, baptism, confirmation, etc.) began in at least the mid-1500s as a result of the Council of Trent. In many cases, parish priests began keeping those sorts of records long before the decree required it. Catholic churches in Portugal were no different.

In 1910, a new government required all church records to be turned over to the national government, and those records are now housed in the National Archives in Lisbon, and some were transferred to state archives in the Districts where the parish resided.

Civil Registration

Civil registration (governmental recording of birth, marriage, death) began in 1870 in Portugal.

National Archives

The National Archives for Portugal is located in Lisboa (Lisbon) – the capital city of Portugal. The archives house a number of historical and genealogical documents for the country. See below for the website. Try as I might, I could find none of them online, however.

District Archives

There are eighteen governmental jurisdictions in Portugal, called districts. Each of them possesses many of the records – ecclesiastical as well as governmental – within their districts. If you are able to identify the town or region your ancestors came from, you may be able to find records relating to them in the archives of that particular district. After reviewing the holdings of a number of districts, I discovered that typical records were held there – birth, death, marriage, as well as baptism and confirmation records.

Helpful Websites for Portuguese Research

Following are websites that will be helpful as you venture into Portugal in search of your ancestors:

Archives of the District of Porto — *www.adporto.pt* – this was one of the better websites I was able to find among the Portuguese districts. Their website is translated into English, and I love their opening paragraph:

> Arquivo Distrital do Porto is alive in a specific space and breathes the air of nowadays. The information and documents in our custody keep the ancient memory that becomes contemporary to guarantee rights and duties, to reveal answers, clarify mysteries, and embrace future adventures.

(Note – if you go beyond the home page, sometimes the translation doesn't occur automatically. If that's the case, click on the icon of the English flag in the upper right-hand corner. If that doesn't work, then use your buddy *Google Translate.*)

Arquivo Nacional Torre do Tombo — *antt.dgarq.gov.pt/* — this is the website for the National Archives located in the Tombo Tower (*Torre do Tombo*). An eclectic gathering of documents is available to search, although most are not online. But addresses for the collections are given, so a letter in Portuguese to the address may result in assistance.

Cyber Pursuits — *www.cyberpursuits.com/gen/iberia.asp* — this is a useful website focused on genealogical research on the Iberian Peninsula, including Portugal. It contains a handful of links to websites that will help you further explore your Portuguese ancestors.

Cyndi's List — *www.cyndislist.com/portugal* -- Cyndi's list has a number of links to websites focusing on doing genealogical research in Portugal.

FamilySearch – *www.familysearch.org* – FamilySearch has a few articles on Portugal, but if you have used FamilySearch for searching other countries, you'll be disappointed in their Portuguese articles and videos collection – they are both very sparse. However, if you don't find an article you are looking for on FamilySearch, Google the topic and see if a FamilySearch article comes up. I found that to be the case on several articles, including an article on church records in Portugal.

They also have a number of Portuguese collections available through microfilm (remember – you can order them to be sent to a Family History Center near you for a nominal fee. They'll arrive at a local LDS meeting-house and will be available for you to view for six weeks). Some of their Portuguese collections are:

• Aveiro Catholic Church Records
• Portugal baptisms
• Portugal marriages
• Portugal deaths
• And about a dozen diocesean records

Tombo — *http://etombo.com/paroquia/agrela.html* — the closest translation I can come up with for this website is "Tumbling" or "falling" (descendants, perhaps?), which probably means there's something lost in my translation! (If any of my readers are fluent in Portuguese and can shed a little light on this, please let me know!) Seriously, I found this to be an excellent website, which provided links to parish records in Portugal. The records were online, and featured images of the documents themselves. I checked a number of the links, and they contained weddings (*casamentos*), births (*naciementos*), deaths (*obitos*), baptisms (*baptismos*), confirmations (*crismados*), etc. One example can be found at: *pesquisa.adporto.pt/cravfrontoffice/?ID=492121*. It is a record of weddings that occurred between November 1701 and May 1747 in Agrela, Santo Tirso.

This website will provide you with a gateway to a number of online records. If you are fortunate, you may be able to find some of your ancestors within its many sources.

Professional Genealogists — *www.fernandocandido.com/portgen/ portresearchers.html* -- if, at the end of the day you are running into brick wall after brick wall, you might contact one of the professional genealogists listed at this website. I cannot vouch for their capabilities, but found them on the Internet, offering their services. I recommend proceeding slowly, define carefully the search you are commissioning, and be very clear about what you are willing to pay. You may try a few smaller searches to try out the genealogist before jumping in with both feet!

If you have been unsuccessful in finding information about your Portuguese ancestors on the various websites listed above, it may be time to reach out to some of the places those records are held. Following are sample letters you might use to request information from the Portuguese authorities. Letters written in English are often discarded and not replied to; therefore you would do better attempting to request those records in Portuguese! Also, I suggest keeping the letters simple and to the point!

June 15, 2013

Good day,

I live in the United States. My ancestors are from Portugal. I would like to learn about them.

Here is the information I have about my ancestors that were born in Portugal:

Last name:

First Name:

Date of birth (approximate):
Place of birth:

Father's given name and surname:

Mother's given name and surname: unknown

I request complete transcriptions of the original records.

Please tell me the cost of these services. The most I want to pay is US$_____. If you send me a bill for the genealogy research, I will pay it. I understand you will not send the information until after I pay.

My address is:
(Enter your mailing address here)

Thank you,

Daniel Quillen
wdanielquillen@gmail.com

Here it is in Portuguese:

15 Junho 2013

Bom dia,

Eu vivo nos Estados Unidos. Meus antepassados eram de Portugal. Eu gostaria de aprender sobre eles.

Eu incluo a informação que tenho sobre meus antepassados que nasceram em Portugal:
Sobrenome:

Nome:

Data de nascimento (aproximado):

Local de Nascimento:

Nome do pai e sobrenome:

Nome e sobrenome da mãe: desconhecido

Eu gostaria que as transcrições completas dos registros originais.

Por favor, deixe-me saber o custo desses serviços. O máximo que eu quero pagar é US$ _____. Se você me enviar um recibo para a pesquisa genealógica. Eu entendo que você não enviar as informações até que depois de eu ter pago.

Meu endereço é:
(Enter your mailing address here)

Obrigado

Daniel Quillen
wdanielquillen@gmail.com

FamilySearch.org has produced a *Portuguese Letter Writing Guide* (*https:// www.familysearch.org/learn/wiki/en/Portuguese_Letter-writing_Guide*) that has some helpful hints and suggestions.

Palavras, palavras, palavras *(Words, words, words)*
Below are words you are likely to run into as you research Portuguese records.
a partir de — from
adulto – adult
ano – year
avó – grandmother
avô — grandfather
batismo – baptism
casado – married

casamento – marriage
cem – hundred
censo – census
certidão de óbito – death certificate
certificado – certificate
civil – civil
crismados – confirmations
dia – day
distrito – district
enterro – burial
esposa – wife
esposo – husband
falecido – deceased
filha – daughter
filho – son
idade – age
Igreja Católica – Catholic Church
irmã — sister
irmão – brother
madrina – godmother
mãe —mother
marido – husband
mês – month
mil – thousand
ministro – minister
morreu – died
mulher – woman
nome — name
nascido – born
nasceu – was born
nascimento – birth
nome de solteira – maiden name
nomeado – named
obitos – deaths
padre – priest
pais – parents
para – to

paróquia — parish
pastor – pastor
registro paroquial — church record
rol – census
sobrenome – surname
tia – aunt
tio — uncle

Meses do Ano (Months of the Year)
Janeiro – January
Fevereiro — February
Março — March
Abril — April
Maio — May
Junho — June
Juhlo — July
Agosto — August
Setembro — September
Outubro — October
Novembro — November
Dezembro — December

Names

Below are first names you are likely to run into as you are researching your Portuguese ancestors. I have found that at least being familiar with the spelling of common names has helped me decipher many genealogy records through the years.

Meninos Portugueses os primeiros nomes (*Portuguese boys' first names*)
Abilio
Adao
Afonso
Bartolmeu
Batista
Caetano
Carlitos

Casimiro
Cornelio
Cristiano
David
Demetrio
Dimas
Dinis
Donato
Duarte
Eleuterio
Eloi
Estevao
Eusebio
Ferrao
Filipe
Gaspar
Goncalo
Graciano
Guilherme
Heitor
Henriques
Hermengildo
Jorge
Josue
Luiz
Manoel

Raparigas Portuguesas primeiros nomes *(Portuguese girls' names)*Amelia
Antonia
Assuncao
Benedita
Candelaria
Carmo
Catarina
Celia
Cintia
Constancia

Domitila
Doroteia
Elisabete
Filomena
Fortunata
Glaucia
Henriqueta
Imaculada
Jacinta
Josefa
Jovita
Ligia
Lurdes
Margarida
Micaela
Nathalia
Neves
Renata
Susana
Teresa
Terezinha
Valeria
Vitoria

13. YOUR SPANISH ROOTS

Welcome to a few pages of Spanish research. If you're like me, most of the Spanish research you run into is for Mexico, or perhaps other locations in Central America or South America. But for those of you whose ancestors came to America from Spain, we'll take a little time and peruse the records from Spain: what they are and how to access them. For sake of simplicity, any references in this chapter about Spanish research are those concerned with researching in Spain.

Key Records

There are a number of key records available as you begin your search for your Spanish roots. Following are some of those sources:

Censuses

Censuses are a hit-and-miss proposition for Spain. No national census has ever been conducted in Spain. The closest they came was between 1749 and 1756 when they conducted a headcount for tax purposes. This was undertaken in the kingdom / autonomous community of Castile and León. It is called the *Marques de Catastro de Ensenada*. For a great explanation and dissertation about these records, go to *FamilySearch.org*, click on the *Search* tab, then click on *Wiki*. In the *Search* box, type *Spain, Cadastre of the Marquis of Ensenada*, and you'll learn all there is to know about these records that are over 250 years old. In a nutshell, they are quasi-census records that include the head of household, his heirs, income, land and assets. FamilySearch.org has digital copies of these records, and the ones I have searched have exquisite handwriting (though difficult to read due to flourishes and an ancient hand!).

While there was no national census, there were local censuses aplenty. These censuses of the local communities (*municipios*) were taken at different times across the width and breadth of the country. Most of the municipios conducted censuses beginning in the late 1800s through present day, but some got started earlier – some as early as the 17th and 18th centuries. Some of these records have been digitized and are available online, but many others are only available by contacting the local municipio or province where the census was taken. A good place to begin seeking these records is in the Ministry of Culture (*Ministerio de Cultura*), which you can find at *www.xmarks.com/site/aer.mcu.es/sgae/index_censo_guia.jsp*. A caution here, though – the entire website is in Spanish, and there is no translation icon. So *www.translate.google* will be your best friend for awhile as you search these pages. Here's a (very) short Spanish tutorial for this website:

Look for *Directorio de Archivos* (Archive Directory); click on it. On the page, you'll see the following terms:

- *Criterios de búsqueda* (Search criteria)
- *Búsqueda General* (General search)
- *Nombre de Archivo*: (Name of archive)
- *Tipo de Archivo: [Seleccion] [Borrar]* (No – Tipo doesn't mean "Tips" the phrase means: File type [Selection] [Clear])

So, if you are looking for records in the province of Cordoba, enter Cordoba in the box below *Búsqueda General*. If you know the town / municipio of the archive, enter that in the box below *Nombre de Archivo*. If you don't know the town, then leave that box blank. Then either hit your return key, or go to the bottom of the page and click *Buscar* (search) or *Limpiar* (clear / reset the page).

Again, if you don't speak Spanish, just use a translation website and muscle your way through. As I did this, I was able to find a lot of information about records that were held in each municipality. Many appear to be only accessible via a visit or a letter requesting assistance. Some sites said there was no librarian available to assist with research; others did offer that service. Many archives records included the names of the director of the library, the address, and some offered e-mail contact.

Municipio = community

Church Records

Well, you knew a predominantly Catholic country like Spain would have a great supply of church records that will assist genealogists, didn't you? The Catholic Church, that great genealogical record keeper through the ages, has not let us down in Spain. Since civil registration did not begin in Spain until 1870, records prior to that are tough to come by outside of Catholic Church records. Among other things, the 16th-century Council of Trent decreed that all Catholic parishes had to keep records of critical events in their parishioners' lives: births, deaths and marriages. And as genealogists, we benefit. In Spain, in general, most Catholic churches began keeping records in the early 1500s, although a few began much earlier – in the 14th century. Many of these records are now online at services like FamilySearch.org and Ancestry.com.

In Spain, most of the Catholic Church's records (baptism / birth, death and marriage) were kept at the parish level. However, most records prior to the 20th century have been centralized into one of seventy diocese locations.

Many diocese records have been microfilmed or digitized by genealogy organizations including FamilySearch.org and Ancestry.com. You can find out information about each diocese and many of the parishes by going to *www.conferenciaepiscopal.es/index.php/la-iglesia-en-espana.html.* Again — this website is in Spanish, so you'll need your translation website friend along for the ride.

As you will find, few Church records have been digitized and placed online. But the LDS Church (as of this writing) has microfilmed close to 40% of the records of the Spanish dioceses. You can either go to Salt Lake City to view them, or request them to be sent to a local Family History Center located in a local LDS meetinghouse.

The website I mentioned in the *Census* section, *www.xmarks.com/site/ aer.mcu.es/sgae/index_censo_guia.jsp,* can locate church records too.

Civil Registration

Civil registration (governmental recording of birth, marriage, death) began in 1870. Prior to that, the only records kept in Spain were kept by the churches, primarily the Catholic Church. These records are all kept by the Minister of Justice (*Ministerio de Justicia*) and genealogical researchers can go to their website: *www.mjusticia.gob.es/cs/Satellite/ en/1200666550194/DetalleInicio.html* and request records online. Unlike many other of the Spanish websites, at least some of

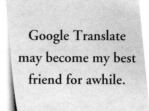

Google Translate may become my best friend for awhile.

this website has an English translation (click on *Welcome* at the top right of the home page). But as you peruse the pages, the English reverts to Spanish.

From the home page, select *Subject Areas*, then select *Registros* (Records), then select *Registro Civil* (Civil Records). By following the various threads, you can discover how to order birth, death and marriage certificates either by mail or via the Internet. To make your request online, you must go to the following page (type carefully!): *https://sede.mjusticia.gob.es/cs/Satellite/ Sede/es/1215197884559/SDTramite/1215327470593/Detalle.html*. (Note — this page takes you to an electronic request for a birth certificate. For a death certificate or a marriage certificate, enter *el certificado de defunción* or *certificado de matrimonio* in the *Buscar* box, then select the page that will instruct you on how to order.)

State Archives

Spain is divided into seventeen governmental divisions called autonomous communities (you'll see them referred to as *comunidades autonomas*) and two autonomous cities. Many of the available genealogical records are located in the archives for each of these communities. The communities / cities are:

Andalucia	Aragon
Asturias	Baleares (Balearic Islands)
Ceuta	Canarias (Canary Islands)
Cantabria	Castilla y León
Castilla-La Mancha	Comunidad Valenciana (Valencian
Cataluna (Catalonia)	Community)
Extremadura	Galicia
La Rioja	Madrid

Melilla   Murcia
Navarra   Pais Vasco (Basque Country)

According to a research guide for Spanish research on FamilySearch.org. the following caveat is listed about several of the communities:

> Note: The autonomous cities of Ceuta and Melilla plus three small islands of Islas Chafarinas, Penon de Alhucemas, and Penon de Velez de la Gomera, administered directly by the Spanish central government, are all along the coast of Morocco and are collectively referred to as Places of Sovereignty (Plazas de Soberania).

Helpful Websites for Spanish Research
Following are websites that will be helpful as you venture into Spain in search of your ancestors:

Ancestry.com
As of this writing, Ancestry.com's international subscription edition includes a brief Spain collection limited to the province of Albacete:

• Albacete province births, 1504 to 1905
• Albacete province marriages, 1504 to 1905

Cyndi's List — *www.cyndislist.com/spain* — Cyndi's list has a number of links to websites focusing on doing genealogical research in Spain.

Directory of Spanish Genealogy — *www.genealogiahispana.com/?language=en* – this website is mostly in Spanish, but Google Translate will help you out with that. At the bottom of the home page, click on *España*, and you'll be taken to a number of links that may assist you with your Spanish research. At the bottom of the page you'll even find the website of a researcher who specializes in genealogical research in Spain (*www.spanish-genealogy.com*).

Spain GenWeb — *www.genealogia-es.com* — this is a great website to begin or continue working on your Spanish research. When you first arrive, you'll most likely note the website is in Spanish. If your ninth grade Spanish doesn't serve you well, just click the *Translate* icon in the top right-hand corner of the website and things should go a little easier for you here.

FamilySearch.org – *www.familysearch.org* has hundreds of articles about Spanish research, and all are available to the public for free. From the home page, click *Search*, then *Wiki*, and type *Spain Research* in the *Search* box, and you'll see such titles as *Spain Research, Catholic Church Records (for many different parishes), Spain, Cadiz passports, Spain Census Records, Spain Websites*, etc.

For most other European countries, FamilySearch has video lessons on doing research in a particular country. I was disappointed to see there were no such videos for research in Spain – *except* three videos on deciphering Spanish handwritten documents. Most of the Spanish documents I have viewed have gorgeous handwriting, but oh-so-tough to interpret. Perhaps one of these videos will assist you. The videos are 20, 25 and 30 minutes, and can be found at *https://www.familysearch.org/learningcenter/results.html?fq=place%3A%22Spain%22*.

Also, at the time of this writing, there are well over 13 million names in FamilySearch's various Spain collections including the following:

• Spain baptisms, 1502 to 1940 (over 8 million death records)
• Spain deaths, 1600 to 1900
• Spain passports for Cádiz, 1810 to 1866
• Spain testaments (wills) for Cádiz, 1550 to 1920
• Spain, Albacete province births, 1504 to 1979

That first collection is an interesting one. I checked it out to see what I could see, and here's a record I was able to locate with a few clicks of a mouse:

Name: Jose Baltasar Lepes Lopez
Gender: Male
Baptism / Christening date: 13 Jan 1869
Baptism / Christening date: Santiago Apostol, Valladolid, Valladolid, Spain
Birth date: 06 Jan 1869

Birthplace: Valladolid
Father's name: Genaro Lepes
Mother's name: Victorina Lopez
Paternal grandfather's name: Juan Miguel Lepes
Paternal grandmother's name: Vicenta Tercero
Maternal grandfather's name: Felis Lopez
Maternal grandmother's name: Tomasa Requena

I think you'll agree that's great information. Not only was I able to locate the baptism or christening date for this Spanish lad, I also discover his parents' and grandparents' names. Good deal!

Genealogy.com Spain Message Boards – *www.genforum.genealogy.com/spain.* This is a great place to visit if you are searching for specific Spanish surnames, have run into a brick wall in any area of research and are looking for some advice on how to proceed, etc. Message boards have long been a great informal tool for genealogists to use, and especially so when they are researching in unfamiliar lands. No sense recreating the wheel if there are those who have been there (along your genealogical path) before and can render assistance.

If you have been unsuccessful in finding information about your Spanish ancestors on the various websites listed above, it may be time to reach out to some of the places those records are held. Following are sample letters you might use to request information from the Spanish authorities. Letters written in English are often discarded and not replied to; therefore you would do better attempting to request those records in Spanish! Also, I suggest keeping the letters simple and to the point!

June 15, 2013

Good day,

I live in the United States. My ancestors are from the Spain. I would like to learn about them.

Here is the information I have about my ancestors that were born in Spain:

Last name:

First Name:

Date of birth (approximate):

Place of birth:

Father's given name and surname:

Mother's given name and surname: unknown

I request complete transcriptions of the original records.

Please tell me the cost of these services. The most I want to pay is US$_____. If you send me a bill for the genealogy research, I will pay it. I understand you will not send the information until after I pay.

My address is:
(Put your mailing address here)

Thank you,

Daniel Quillen
wdanielquillen@gmail.com

And in Spanish:

15 Junio 2013

Buenos días,

Yo vivo en los Estados Unidos. Mis antepasados fueron de España. Me gustaría aprender sobre ellos.

Aquí incluyo la información que tengo sobre mis antepasados que nacieron en España:

Apellido:

Nombre:

Fecha de nacimiento (aproximada):

Lugar de nacimiento:

Nombre del padre y apellidos:

Nombre de la madre y apellidos: desconocido

Pido las transcripciones completas de los registros originales.

Por favor, avíseme del costo de estos servicios. Lo más que quiero pagar es US$ _____. Si usted me envía una cuenta para cobrar la investigación de la genealogía, la pagaré. Entiendo que Ud. no enviará la información hasta después de que yo pague.

Mi dirección es:
(Put your mailing address here)

Gracias,

Daniel Quillen
wdanielquillen@gmail.com

FamilySearch.org has produced a *Spanish Letter Writing Guide* (*https://www.familysearch.org/learn/wiki/en/images/a/aa/LWGSpanish.pdf*) that has helpful hints and suggestions. If you want to be a little more specific in your address than *Buenos Dias*, following are some possibilities they recommend:

Dear Sir:	Estimado señor:
Dear Father:	Estimado Reverendo Padre:
Your Excellency*	Su Excelencia:

Note that using "Your Excellency" as a form of address is most appropriate for a Catholic bishop or archbishop

If you can find an e-mail address for the particular archive or parish address you are seeking, that will of course expedite your request. Otherwise, you need to ferret out the address for the facility.

Palabras, palabras, palabras *(Words, words, words)*
Below are words you are likely to run into as you research records.

año — year
apellido – surname
archive – archive
bautismo – baptism
censo – census
certificado de defunción – death certificate
certificado de matrimonio – marriage certificate
certificado de nacimiento – birth certificate
ciento – hundred
confirmación — confirmation
crisma — confirmation
dia – day
entierro — burial
esposa – wife
esposo – husband
Iglesia Católica – Catholic Church
matrimonio – marriage
madre – mother
mesa—month
mil – thousand
muerte – death
mujer – wife
nacimiento – birth
niño — child

nombre – name
nombre de pila – given name
padre – priest
padres – parents
pai – father
parroquia – parish
registros civil – civil records
registros parroquiales — church records
sepultura – burial

Meses del año *(Months of the Year)*
Enero – January
Febrero — February
Marzo — March
Abril — April
Mayo — May
Junio — June
Julio — July
Agosto — August
Septiembre -- September
Octubre — October
Noviembre — November
Deciembre — December

Names
Below are first names you are likely to run into as you research your Spanish ancestors. I have found that at least being familiar with the spelling of common names has helped me decipher many genealogy records.

Nombres de los niños españoles primeros *(Spanish boys' first names)*
Abran
Adan
Alano
Alejandro
Amistad
Antonio
Bartoli

Beltran
Carlo
Caton
Cid
Dante
Desiderio
Diego
Emilio
Estefan
Evardo
Fernando
Gilberto
Hector
Hidalgo
Inocencio
Isaias
Jacinto
Joaquin
Jose
Katia
Lonzo
Luciano
Marco
Milagro
Nesto
Pacual

Chicas españolas nombres de pila *(Spanish girls' first names)*
Adalia
Adoncia
Alandra
Amaranta
Aquila
Bebe
Bonita
Cailida
Chalina

Consuelo
Dulcinea
Elisa
Engracia
Esperanza
Jaira
Jardena
Lolita
Mahogany
Marisol
Mira
Nelia
Novia
Othelia
Paloma
Piedad
Raseda
Sancia
Shaba
Soledad
Suela
Valencia
Vallia
Zelia

INDEX

GENEALOGICAL NOTES

GENEALOGICAL NOTES

GENEALOGICAL NOTES

COLD SPRING PRESS GENEALOGY BOOKS

Secrets of Tracing Your Ancestors, 5th Edition, $12.95
The Troubleshooter's Guide to Do-It-Yourself Genealogy, 2nd Edition,
$14.95

Quillen's **Essentials of Genealogy** series offers the following books:
• *Mastering Online Genealogy*, $9.95
• *Mastering Immigration & Naturalization Records*, $9.95
• *Mastering Census & Military Records*, $9.95
• *Tracing Your European Roots*, $11.95
• *Tracing Your Irish & British Roots*, $9.95
• *Mastering Family, Library, & Church Records*, $9.95

All our books available in major bookstores, online booksellers, or
through our website at **www.essentialgenealogy.com**.